Stitched Blooms

Stitched Blooms

300 Floral, Leaf & Border Motifs to Embroider

Carina Envoldsen-Harris

LARK

An Imprint of Sterling Publishing
387 Park Avenue South
New York, NY 10016

ISBN 978-1-4547-0425-6

Envoldsen-Harris, Carina.
 Stitched blooms : 300 floral, leaf, & border motifs to embroider / Carina Envoldsen-Harris.
    pages cm
 ISBN 978-1-4547-0425-6
 1. Embroidery--Patterns. 2. Decoration and ornament--Plant forms. I. Title.
 TT773.E58 2013
 746.44--dc23

                                  2012049426

Distributed in Canada by Sterling Publishing
c/o Canadian Manda Group, 165 Dufferin Street
Toronto, Ontario, Canada M6K 3H6
Distributed in the United Kingdom by GMC Distribution Services
Castle Place, 166 High Street, Lewes, East Sussex, England BN7 1XU
Distributed in Australia by Capricorn Link (Australia) Pty. Ltd.
P.O. Box 704, Windsor, NSW 2756, Australia

For information about custom editions, special sales, and premium and corporate purchases, please contact Sterling Special Sales at 800-805-5489 or specialsales@sterlingpublishing.com.

Email academic@larkbooks.com for information about desk and examination copies.
The complete policy can be found at larkcrafts.com.

Manufactured in China

2 4 6 8 10 9 7 5 3 1

larkcrafts.com

Contents

Introduction

Flowers are endlessly inspiring to me. The variety in shapes, sizes, color, and pattern is just incredible. You couldn't make up this variety even if you tried. Since I can remember, I've always been drawn to flowers and to drawing them.

If I could have one super power, I would like to be able to make flowers appear anywhere. Alas, I do not have that power, but I can stitch flowers on any (inanimate) surface that will stand still for long enough.

The 300 motifs in this book are an eclectic mix of real and imaginary flowers, plus a few other growing things. You'll find folk-art inspired flowers, minimalist flower motifs, blouse-y flowers, and anything in between. I've included some lovely leaves, because a flower without leaves is like wearing a fancy frock without any shoes on. A few berries and nuts have also sneaked in. There are flowery and leafy borders, too!

You can use the motifs straight out of the book pages or take advantage of the enclosed CD, which has all of the motifs in black and white. Adjust and combine them however you like, by changing the size of the motifs or by adding or removing elements. Step-by-step instructions are included for downloading and sizing the motifs from the CD, so you can stitch them to nearly anything you'd like!

For even more fun, you'll find 20 projects beginning on page 34 that feature many of the motifs in this book. Whether you'd like to stitch up a handy sewing kit in which to stash your embroidery tools, need some pretty little luminary bags to light up your home, or want to spiff up an old skirt with embroidered foliage, you'll find lots of ways to get inspired.

But don't let my imagination be the limit to the flora you can stitch! I have included ideas for how you can turn the flowers in your own garden, or elsewhere, into motifs. Mix and match your own designs with the motifs in this book to make something truly unique. No matter how you choose to use this book, let your imagination guide you, and enjoy!

Color inspires me a lot. As much as I love pattern, I sometimes wonder if the reason I embroider is because it gives me a reason to play with color. After all, the patterns only really come to life when color is added!

You can find color inspiration in many places: a skirt in your wardrobe, a favorite blanket, postage stamps, posters, and of course in nature. Choosing color is part science and part magic. The science part can be explained, but the magic is a bit harder to put into words.

Color Stuff

Okay, I'm not going to get all that scientific—there are no fancy formulas or anything here. But there are some givens that explain why things work the way they do in the world of color.

Basic Color Theory

Chances are you have come across the color wheel a few times. Perhaps in school you were taught about primary colors and how to mix secondary and tertiary colors.

Quick color mixing reminder: The three primary colors—red, yellow, and blue—cannot be made from other colors. But with the primary colors, you can mix all other colors. The secondary colors are orange (red + yellow), green (yellow + blue), and violet (blue + red). There are six tertiary colors, each mixed from a primary and a secondary color: red-orange, yellow-orange, yellow-green, blue-green, blue-violet, and red-violet.

Perhaps the color wheel lesson in school only went as far as how to mix colors. That's often the case, and it's a real shame because the color wheel can help us a lot when selecting colors. Of course, there is an infinite number of colors in the world, and they would obviously not fit on a color wheel, so the wheel is a simplified model of color mixing.

Mixing is perhaps not the best word to use when talking about the relationship between colors in embroidery, because we can't physically mix two colors of stranded floss. No matter how tightly you twist them together, red floss and yellow floss will not turn orange—they will always remain red or yellow. But they may look orange from some distance and that is very important to keep in mind.

Colors are very much influenced by their neighbors. Yellow and red next to each other will make each other look slightly orange. The same thing goes for any color; if there's another color sitting next to it, they will impact each other, even if just a little bit. This can create unfortunate, unwanted effects, like a yellow that looks very nice on its own, but when placed next to a green takes on a green tinge.

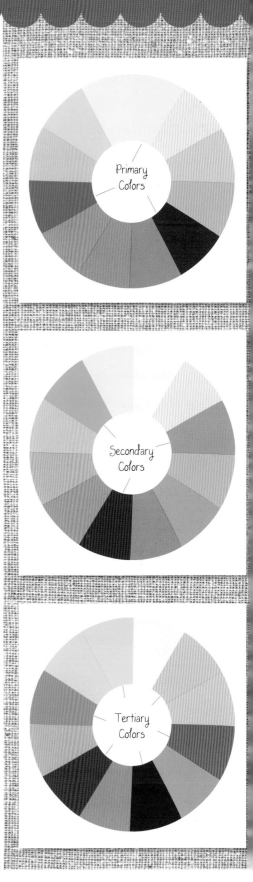

Value (Light and Dark)

Warm and Cool

But we can also use this effect to our advantage, to make it look like we've used more colors than we actually have, much like Impressionist painters who often would mix colors not on the palette but by putting small dots or strokes of paint next to each other on the canvas, creating the illusion of a third color. This is called partitive or optical mixing. And we can do something similar with thread colors!

Imagine using a monochrome palette for your embroidery pattern—blue, for example—and then adding just a few yellow stitches. This will add another dimension to your colors, because where the blue and yellow get close to each other, subconsciously we will be seeing green. We may not actually be seeing it, but the effect is there.

VALUE (LIGHT AND DARK)
Something that can have great impact on the overall color choices for a stitched piece is the value of the thread colors—not how much you paid for them, but how light or dark they are. This can sometimes seem tricky to determine because, although two colors look very different, they may actually have the same, or nearly the same, value. Take, for example, a red and a green. We're so used to thinking of them as very different from each other; they're complementary colors after all, placed across from each other on the color wheel. And yet, in terms of value, they are very close to each other.

One way to determine the values in a color selection is to take a photograph of the colors. Take either a black-and-white photo, or a color photo that you can change to grayscale with a photo-editing program on your computer. Then it should be quite clear which colors are light, medium, or dark. Value matters, because if we only use colors with similar values, the piece can seem flat and dull. But using similar values can also make a piece look calm, which may be exactly the effect you want sometimes.

Some colors are naturally light, like yellow, for instance. It is impossible to have a yellow that falls at the dark end of the value spectrum. Similarly, some colors tend to be naturally dark, like violet and blue, while others fall in the medium range. Of course, if a color has been mixed with another color, or with black or white, the value can change.

WARM AND COOL
Colors are either warm or cool. Yellow, orange, and red (and the colors in between them) are generally considered warm colors, while green, blue, and violet are cool colors. But all is not what it seems! The colors we usually think of as warm can be cool, and vice versa. This is especially true for the primary colors. Secondary and tertiary colors usually start to seem muddy if you try to change their temperature by mixing in another color. But the primaries are a different story. Mix just a tiny

bit of red with a blue and that blue has become a warm blue. Or add a minuscule amount of blue to yellow and it is now a cool yellow.

Why does it matter whether a color is warm or cool? Because of how the atmosphere affects how we see color, cooler colors seem farther away than warmer colors. This can be used in art and design to create a 3-D effect. Consider a traditional landscape painting: The far background will usually be blues, greens, and violets, whereas the foreground has more warm colors, such as terracotta, burnt umber, and yellow. This makes the landscape painting feel three-dimensional, like we would see it in real life. Warm colors advance toward you, and cool colors recede.

And although the advancing/receding effect isn't quite as pronounced in embroidery as it is in quilting, for example (unless you're using a lot of fill stitching), it will still subtly affect the final outcome. The warm colors will "pop" a bit more than the cooler ones.

Color Schemes

If we go back to the color wheel, we can use it as a reminder of color schemes that usually work well together—depending on individual tastes, of course. Although yellow and violet (complementary colors) should make an interesting pair, I'm just not that into those colors.

MONOCHROMATIC

Monochrome means "one color"; a monochromatic color scheme is one that uses a single color plus any variation of that color mixed with black or white. Strictly speaking, a monochromatic scheme isn't on the color wheel, but it can still be very effective. It can be subtle if you use a monochromatic scale with similar values, or more dramatic if you use values from both ends of the spectrum.

COMPLEMENTARY

A complementary color scheme has more "zing" than the others. This is because it uses just two colors that are on the opposite sides of the color wheel, a primary and a secondary color (though you can use other pairings, too). The reason these combinations are so forceful is that they have nothing in common. Take a blue-orange pair, for example: The orange is made from yellow and red, and has no blue in it; blue is of course only made of itself. It's the maximum contrast. So if you want a color scheme that can be almost aggressive, try a complementary one!

HARMONIZING

When you want something calmer, try a harmonizing scheme. This scheme also uses only two colors, but they are located right next to each other on the color wheel. Take yellow and orange, for example: They have a lot in common and the main contrast between them would be their values. As the name implies, you will have harmony with this scheme.

Monochromatic

Complementary

Harmonizing

Analogous

Split Complementary

Triadic

ANALOGOUS

An analogous color scheme is also fairly calm, but there is a bit more contrast. This scheme is made up of three colors (sometime more) in a row on the color wheel. It is a pleasant scheme because the colors are close together; however, the ones on the edges that are farther apart add more contrast, especially if you use value to your advantage.

SPLIT COMPLEMENTARY

As the name suggests, this is not a true complementary scheme. Instead of using two colors directly opposite one another on the color wheel, you use one color with the two colors on either side of its opposite, so there are three colors in the scheme. For example, instead of red and green, you will have red and blue-green plus yellow-green. There is still a fairly big contrast, but it's not quite as dramatic as a pure complementary scheme.

TRIADIC

In a triadic color scheme, the colors are spaced evenly on the color wheel. It's a bit like a complementary scheme, because the colors may not necessarily have anything in common. But because there are three colors, they are closer together, which makes the scheme more balanced and the contrast between them less pronounced.

COLOR MAGIC

Where does the color magic come from? It's a combination of instinct and knowledge. Maybe you chose a particular palette very deliberately by using the color wheel for maximum contrast. Maybe you chose it because it just felt right; you saw that combination on an old postcard or a quilt and you were inspired! Afterward, you might analyze the colors, and it often turns out that a color selection is related to one of the color schemes mentioned.

Being "good" at putting colors together can be practiced. The more you work with colors, the better you will get at combining them. You can train yourself by challenging the color choices you make. And always think about why certain combinations do or don't work well.

These are some of the color combinations I often use:
* Aqua, orange-yellow, pink, yellow, orange-red
* Orange, yellow-orange, red, grass green, sky blue
* Sky blue, magenta, teal, aqua, lime green
* Lime green, forest green, sky blue, orange-red, pink
* Orange, yellow, violet, lilac, orange-red
* Light to medium blues with a contrasting orange color
* Lime green, grass green, aqua, orange, lilac

Looking at the palettes I usually put together, I can tell that they often are split-complementary or triadic color schemes. I like when colors play against each other but are not necessarily complete opposite colors. The colors are usually also quite saturated—it's rare that I use anything in earth tones or pastels. Maybe your choices are similar, or perhaps you like the more muted colors or maybe full-on complementary colors.

As you start to notice which colors often pop up, you can build a go-to palette that you know will work for you. This is especially handy because you will know what colors you always need in your stash.

Color Exploration Exercises

* Restrict the number of colors in a project to two or three. This will force you to explore the relationship between the colors. Use more of one color and it will impact your work in one way; use more of another color and it will have a different effect.

* Use colors you don't normally gravitate toward. This can be tricky because it's so easy to disregard the positive effects of a color that you don't like. But it can be done!

* Ask someone else to pick colors for you. Again, this is a tricky one, because not everyone has the same taste in color. Make the selection work, even if you don't particularly like it.

* Put together a selection of colors you really like, then replace one of the colors with its complementary color. What happened? Did you like this new combination?

Fabric & Thread

To embroider, you will of course need thread and fabric. With free-form embroidery, as in this book, you can use pretty much any type of fabric you like: quilting cotton, felt, linen, whatever. Unlike counted thread stitching, the design of the stitching isn't determined by the surface, so no one fabric is better or worse than any other. Likewise with thread: You can use any type you like, though some types of thread go better with some types of fabric than others. For example, stitching on a thick knitted fabric with 6-stranded floss may not be such a good idea because the thread will sink into the fabric. But sometimes even threads and fabrics that aren't the ideal combination will give interesting results. Experimenting is always fun!

PREPARING FABRIC

It is important to wash fabrics before stitching on them. This will remove any residual dye or sizing, but more importantly, it will preshrink the fabric. If you stitch on unwashed fabric, then wash it, it might shrink and distort the stitching. It may even be so bad that the whole thing is ruined. Oh dear! Of course, if your project is never going to be washed, it doesn't matter as much, but it's a good habit nonetheless! Ironing the fabric before stitching on it will also make the end result neater.

CARING FOR STITCHED PIECES

Although a lot of embroidery thread is suitable for washing, it is still worth taking a lot of care when doing so. Washing by hand is the gentlest way to clean your stitcheries, but some projects may be easiest to wash in a machine. In such cases, wash at a low temperature and preferably on a delicate cycle. And always check the directions supplied by the manufacturer of the thread used; some threads are designated as dry-clean only.

Tip

If your finished stitches become flattened, you can plump them up by running slightly damp fingertips across the stitched areas. Take care not to catch any thread with your fingernails.

IRONING

Before ironing embroidered areas, always make sure that all transfer lines have been rinsed out completely. If they are not, they can be set permanently by the heat of the iron. Also, be sure to iron embroidery on the reverse side of the fabric and lay it on top of a clean white towel, to prevent the stitches from being completely flattened. If you find it necessary to iron the embroidered fabric from the front, use a lower setting and don't press down too hard.

Threads

There are many types of thread that can be used for embroidery. It all depends on the effect you want to achieve and the fabric you are stitching on. The projects in this book are mostly stitched using 6-stranded cotton, but perle cotton and crewel wool have been used too.

There are many different brands of thread. Some brands focus on just one type of thread, while others make a whole range of different threads. There will be slight differences between how each brand makes a certain type of thread, so it's a good idea to try different ones to see which you prefer, whether for the color range, the way the thread feels, or the sheen of it.

Perle (or pearl) cotton is a twisted, 2-ply thread with a high sheen. It comes in five sizes or weights. The higher the number, the finer the thread. Perle cotton is used as is, and is not meant to be split into strands.

Crewel wool is a fine 2-ply yarn made of wool. Crewel wool is also used as is and not meant to be split into strands.

Embroidery floss, or 6-strand, is loosely twisted 6-strand thread. It is usually made from cotton and is slightly glossy. Rule of thumb: if the floss has no sheen or gloss at all, then the quality probably isn't great. The better the quality, the less the thread will tangle and tie itself into knots. Six-strand comes in both solid colors and in color variations, which are multi-colored shades.

Embroidery floss is also made from a variety of other materials, such as silk, linen, metallic, and synthetic. DMC has a wide range of these specialty flosses, and they are great to use when you want to give your work a little something extra. They are not as easy to use as regular cotton floss, because they split easily and can be difficult to thread. But it is well worth the effort to have flashes of gold or fluorescent green.

Using 6-Stranded Floss

SEPARATING STRANDS

Separating 6-strand floss is easier than it might look. At a cut end of a length of floss, separate the desired number of strands from the rest and then gently pull the two sections apart. Pull them as straight as possible, not at an angle. They should separate easily, but if they do start to tangle, hold on to the two sections with your ring and little fingers and untangle the floss with the rest of your fingers.

STRIPPING FLOSS

It is almost impossible to keep your floss completely tangle-free, but an easy way to make it less tangly is to strip the floss. This means separating all 6 strands and then putting the required number of strands back together again. Run a couple of fingers down the length of the new bundle of strands to make sure they stay together.

LENGTH OF THREAD TO USE

There are no rules for how long your thread should be—it depends on your preferences. Maybe you like a fairly short thread, or perhaps a longer one. Of course, using a very short thread—less than 8 inches (20.3 cm)—means you'll be needing more thread very quickly. On the other hand, anything over 20 inches (50.8 cm) is very likely to twist and knot itself, and that is not good at all. If your thread is around 13 to 15 inches (33 to 38.1 cm), that is a good length. You might want to start there, and adjust to a length you prefer.

UNTWISTING THREAD: THE DANGLE METHOD

As you stitch away on your project, the thread will inevitably start to tangle a little bit—sometimes a lot! This is especially the case when the stitches you use are quite twisty; for instance, French knots and chain stitches. But you can easily untangle the thread. Simply hold up the hoop with your work (if you're using a hoop; otherwise simply hold up your fabric) and let the needle and thread dangle from it. The needle will turn by itself and untwist the thread.

THREAD HEAVEN

Thread Heaven is a great thing to have in your sewing supplies. It's a tiny box with a substance that resembles wax. You use it by pulling your thread through it. Coating the thread will help when threading your needle and makes the thread less likely to tangle. It is especially useful when using fancy threads, such as metallics.

Embroidery Tools

A needle, a hoop or two, a pair of scissors—embroidery tools are inexpensive and are easily found in most craft stores. Following is a list of items you'll need to complete the projects in this book. Gather them all together, read through the instructions on how to use them, and you'll be stitching in no time!

Pattern Transfer Tools

There are numerous ways you can transfer embroidery patterns to fabric. Not all transfer methods are suitable for every type of fabric, and the color of the fabric can also influence which method to use.

WATER-SOLUBLE FABRIC PEN

This is my favorite method of transferring patterns. It is very simple, and you don't have to fiddle with reversing patterns first. Tape the pattern to a window or light table, then tape your fabric on top of the pattern and trace the pattern with a water-soluble fabric pen or marker. Don't worry if your tracing lines are a bit wobbly and not precisely like the pattern; you can adjust the lines as you stitch. Once you're done stitching, gently rinse the piece until all the tracing lines have disappeared. This method is best for light-colored fabrics that aren't too heavy. If the fabric is somewhat translucent when held up to a window in daylight, it should be fine.

IRON-ON PENCIL

You can make your own iron-on transfers by using an iron-on pen or pencil. Trace the pattern onto a piece of paper (printer paper will do) with the pen or pencil. Place the paper on top of the fabric with the tracing facing the fabric. Press the back of the paper to transfer the tracing. When you use this method, remember to reverse the pattern before tracing it with the pencil. The iron-on lines are permanent, so they must be covered completely by the stitching. This method can be used on most colors of fabric; just use a pencil in a color that contrasts with the fabric. Iron-on pencils come in a few different colors, so there will be one that shows up on the color of most fabrics.

TRANSFER, GRAPHITE, OR CARBON PAPER

This tissue-like paper has color on one side. Place the paper on the fabric with the color side facing down. Place the pattern on top and trace with a blunt instrument, such as a tracing stylus or a crochet hook. There is no need to reverse the pattern when using this method. The paper comes in several colors and can be bought in sheets or

rolls. The transfer lines can be rinsed out, but make sure that they are completely gone; if you iron the lines, they can set permanently on the fabric. Transfer paper can be used on most types of fabric and on a lot of other materials, such as leather.

TISSUE PAPER

Using tissue paper to transfer a pattern is especially good for fabrics that are thick or have a lot of texture. It's a good option when none of the other methods will "stick" to the fabric, and is very good when stitching on felt. Place the tissue paper on top of the pattern and trace it with a pen or pencil, then baste the tissue paper to your fabric and stitch the pattern. When you're done, carefully tear away the paper. Any little bits that may be stuck under the stitching can be removed with tweezers or the tip of a needle.

OTHER TRANSFER METHODS

Some other transfer options are as follows:

* You can use a pencil just like you would a water-soluble pen, but you will need to cover the lines completely as it may not be possible to remove them.
* You can use a printer or copier to make an iron-on transfer, but it must be a laser printer/copier, which uses carbon to make the print.
* You can use regular paper in the same way as tissue paper to transfer a pattern, but the stitching will be slightly looser. Also, removing the paper will take extra patience because it doesn't tear as easily as tissue paper.

Needles & Pins

There are many types of needles—some very specialized, some general purpose. All the projects in this book have been stitched with a size 6 or 7 crewel needle.

A couple of types of needles you might want to have in your sewing kit are crewel and tapestry.

CREWEL OR EMBROIDERY NEEDLES

These come in several sizes, numbered from 3 to 10: the higher the number, the finer the needle. Sizes 9 and 10 are used for fine embroidery, with silk for example, or with 1 to 2 strands of stranded floss. Sizes 3 to 8 are more general-purpose needles. Use them with 3 to 6 strands of stranded floss or perle cotton no. 8 and no. 12. You can also use them as sewing needles. They are fairly easy to thread because they have large eyes. The point of a crewel needle is sharp, meant to pierce a hole in the fabric.

TAPESTRY OR CROSS-STITCH

These also come in different sizes, numbered from 12 to 28, and again: the higher the number, the finer the needle. Sizes 22 to 28 are commonly used for cross-stitch and 12 to 20 for wool embroidery (with tapestry wool, for example) and ribbon embroidery. Tapestry needles have blunt points because they are mainly used on even-weave fabric, which already has "holes" in it. The blunt points enable the needles to go through the fabric without catching.

When picking a needle for a project, you want to keep two things in mind: the thickness of the thread and the job the needle will perform. If the thread is thick, then your needle must have a large eye. If you use a needle with an eye that is too small for the thread, you will have trouble pulling the thread through the fabric. But the eye mustn't be so large that it will leave a visible hole around the thread in the fabric. If the needle has to pierce the fabric, then you need a needle with a sharp point.

CARING FOR YOUR NEEDLES

Look after your needles and they will last for years. Keep them away from moisture or they may rust. It is a good idea to have a pincushion with emery sand; this will keep your needles sharp and will also help remove any rust. If you don't have a pincushion with emery, an emery board (yes, like the ones you use to file your nails) is also a handy tool for removing any burrs from the tips of your needles. If your favorite needle starts to curve slightly, do not be alarmed. It has simply formed to the way you use it, and as long as it's still comfortable to use, all is well. However, if the needle is actually bent, then it may be time to get a new needle; usually attempting to straighten a needle results in breaking it.

PINCUSHION

A pincushion is a really good thing to have. It will keep your needles and pins safe, and if you always use your pincushion you won't have to worry about needles disappearing into the armrest of your chair or dropping on the floor.

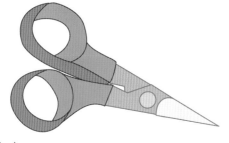

Scissors

A good pair of scissors is indispensable when embroidering. Don't skimp on your scissors—buy the best you can afford. There are many brands of scissors. If possible, try a few different ones to find one that suits you best. But the most important thing about a pair of embroidery scissors is that the point is very sharp, so you don't risk cutting what you don't mean to cut.

Fabric scissors should be fairly long, so you can cut a good length of fabric at a time. Make sure that the scissors are not too heavy and that they're comfortable in your hand.

Tip

Mark your embroidery and fabric scissors so the rest of your family doesn't use them. Tie a bit of brightly colored thread to the handle of your embroidery scissors and a small piece of fabric to the handle of the fabric scissors. And inform the family that these scissors are for your use only!

Hoops

Embroidery hoops (sometimes called frames) are not absolutely necessary. Most of the time using a hoop is a good thing. It will keep your fabric taut and easier to stitch. But you can stitch without one. And in some cases hoops can be a hindrance. For example, doing a lot of running stitches is easier without a hoop. And if your fabric is quite thick or stiff, a hoop will not be suitable.

Hoops come in many different shapes: round, oval, square, and oblong, in sizes that start at 3 inches (7.6 cm) in diameter. Some hoops are made from wood, others from plastic. You do not need a hoop of every size and shape. A couple of round hoops will do to start with. A 4-inch (10.2 cm) diameter will fit most smaller patterns, and 7 inches (17.8 cm) should be large enough for most other patterns you will come across.

To hoop your fabric, separate the two hoop rings and place the fabric on top of the inner ring (the one without a screw). Then place the outer ring on top and tighten the screw to secure it around the inner ring and fabric. Gently pull at the fabric all along the edges to make sure the fabric is taut. Don't make it so taut that it becomes springy.

When you know you will not be working on your embroidery for several days, remove the fabric from the hoop. Leaving it in the hoop may stretch the fabric permanently, and you'll end up with a hoop-shaped crease that can be very difficult to remove. It may also be a good idea to bind at least one of the hoop rings, usually the inner ring, with twill tape. This will help keep the fabric taut for longer. The padding also gives a little extra protection for the fabric.

Attach the twill tape to the ring with a clothespin and then wind the tape around the ring. The edges of the tape should line up but not overlap. Overlapping will create bumpy ridges. Adjust the tape as you go. When you come back to where you started, cut off excess tape and sew it together with the beginning of the tape. Sew along one edge of the ring, not the circumference.

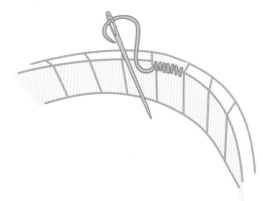

Stabilizers

Not all fabrics are easy to embroider on. For example, T-shirts can be a real pain to stitch because of the knitted fabric they are made from. But there's a solution! Fabric stabilizers add support for delicate fabrics and stabilize stretchy fabrics. There are four main types, listed below. Regardless of which type of stabilizer you use, make sure to read the instructions from the manufacturer so you don't ruin your fabric or stitching.

* Cut-away is a permanent stabilizer that remains on the fabric once you're done stitching. It keeps the fabric from stretching during stitching or wash and wear. Once stitching is done, rough-cut excess stabilizer and then trim the rest close to the stitching with sharp embroidery scissors.
* Tear-away is a temporary stabilizer that is completely removed once stitching is done. Tear-away can be attached with temporary fabric adhesive or by basting. Always take care when removing it from the stitching as it can pull the stitches.
* Heat-away stabilizer is temporary and is often used for delicate fabrics that can't be washed or would rip if you used tear-away. Baste heat-away to the fabric. Once done with the stitching, the stabilizer is removed using a dry iron.
* Wash-away stabilizer is temporary. It is available in different types: plastic-like film, paper, and spray-on liquids. The film and paper types are basted on. Wash-away is removed by washing or rinsing the fabric.

Interfacing

Interfacing is used on the wrong side of a fabric to make it more rigid. It can seem like an impossible task to pick the right interfacing. There are two main types, which both come in different versions, weights, and even color!

The two types are sew-in interfacing and fusible interfacing. Sew-in is especially good for very textured fabric, napped fabric (e.g., velvet), loose or open-weave fabric, and heat sensitive fabrics (e.g., vinyl and sequins). For most other fabrics, fusible (or iron-on) interfacing can be used.

The different versions of interfacing include woven, nonwoven, and knit:

* Non-woven can be cut in any direction because it has no grain, and it won't unravel either. It is not suitable, however, for knit fabrics.
* Woven interfacing has lengthwise and crosswise grain, so you must make sure to match its grain with that of your fabric. This also doesn't work well with knit fabrics.
* Knit interfacing is suitable for stretchy, knit fabrics such as jersey. Because this interfacing is knitted too, it will move with the fabric.

The weights of interfacing are light, medium, and heavy. Always match the weight of the interfacing with the weight of the fabric. If you use an interfacing that is heavier than the fabric, it will add an unnatural stiffness.

Interfacing usually comes in two colors: light/white and dark/black. Use the color that is closest to your fabric. If you use dark interfacing with light or loosely woven fabric it may show through. The same goes for using light interfacing with dark fabrics; it may not show through, but it might affect the appearance of the color of the fabric.

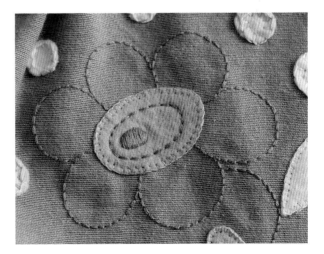

Working with Motifs

Inspiration for embroidery designs can come from many places. I am especially inspired by nature: flowers, leaves, swirling tendrils, and so on. But patterns and colors in other places are also sources of inspiration.

Finding Inspiration

You'll find three hundred motifs in this book! The Project section contains 33 motifs, and an additional 267 motifs can be found in the Motif section. All of the project motifs are at 100 percent, unless otherwise specified. Black and white versions of all 300 motifs are included on the CD. Project motifs are categorized under their project's names. They are available as PDFs, which are sized to fit the project; as EPS files that can be saved to your computer to import into imaging software of your choice to enlarge, rotate, and edit; and as JPEGs, which can be used as is. Motifs from the Motif Section can be found under their section name and corresponding number. They are available as both EPS files that can be modified to your needs, and as JPEGs, which can be used as is.

Whether you choose to use the motifs straight out of the book or from the CD, you can adapt most, if not all of them, to suit your projects. You can do this with a program on your computer, or print out the motifs to cut apart and arrange just how you like them to look. The embroidered blouse on page 99 is an example of mixing and matching: The pattern is actually made up of several smaller motifs. Select motifs and, if necessary, change the sizes to suit the area you want to stitch. Many of the border motifs have corresponding corners, but you can also make up your own pairings. One possibility is to super-size a corner motif to make it stand out.

Finding inspiration for your own motifs and patterns is a lot easier than you might think. Go for a walk, whether in the city or the countryside. Inspiration is everywhere, if only you look for it. Take a camera with you, or a sketchbook, if that's more your thing—I love using a sketchbook. You don't need a fancy camera; the one in a mobile/cell phone will do. It's not about taking artsy photos; it's about documenting your inspiration.

Look for pleasing color inspirations in peeling paint, rusting fences, or a dress in a shop window. Study painted houses, the color of leaves against a blue sky, or maybe a sky laden with thunderclouds. Color is everywhere!

Motifs are everywhere, too! Notice the way a plant twists itself around a lamppost, wrought-iron decorations on an old door, painted floor tiles, the tablecloth you use every day. Look for ideas in China plates, the skirt of a random lady on the street, bark on a tree, and so many, many more places.

Photograph (or draw) the things that catch your eye. Don't think too much about the photos themselves, just snap away, not worrying about making it look good. Even if a photo is slightly blurry, all isn't lost!

When you come home, look through the photos and pick those you like best—or maybe the ones you like least, to give yourself a challenge! Print the photos and then trace those parts that appeal to you onto another piece of paper. That's the starting point of your pattern. Transfer your design to fabric and start stitching, and add things as you go along, if you feel like it. Or don't stitch some elements, if that feels right.

Inspiration can also be found in places other than a walk. Go to a museum, watch a film, go to the library, or look through books and magazines. The Internet, of course, is full of pretty pictures to be inspired by (but don't copy them outright; it's bad karma to copy other people's work, after all).

Embroidery Techniques

No one wants to spend time creating a lovely stitched piece, only to realize the hem is fraying, lumps are visible from the back, or seams are unraveling. These simple techniques will ensure your work looks its best for years to come!

Appliqué

Appliqué is a great way to quickly add both color and texture to a project. There are two basic types: raw edge and needle-turned.

raw-edge appliqué

In raw-edge appliqué, the cutout fabric pieces are sewn onto the base fabric without doing anything else to them. You can use fusible webbing to adhere them to the base first, but it's not strictly necessary. Especially small pieces will do fine with just the stitching. Use small straight stitches perpendicular to the edge of the appliqué patch. You can also use other more decorative stitches, for example the blanket stitch (page 31) or even the cross-stitch (page 29). As long as the stitches go through both the base and the appliqué patch and secure the latter to the former, any stitch goes! Raw-edge will, as the name suggests, leave the edges raw and exposed to wear. They will eventually fray a little, giving the piece a soft, used look—less so if you use fusible webbing.

Needle-turned appliqué is a bit more time consuming, but will give you a neater look and the edges will not

fray. If the fabric shape you wish to appliqué is meant for needle-turned, remember to add seam allowance (or turning allowance) when you cut out the shapes, typically ¼ inch (6 mm). Here's what you do:

needle-turned appliqué

1 Mark the seam allowance on the right side of the patches to help keep an even edge, using a water-soluble pen.

2 Cut out your patches and pin or baste them in place on the fabric. If the patches have curves, clip along these to help make the edge smooth. The clips should only be ⅛ inch (3 mm) long.

3 Bring the needle up from the back of the base fabric somewhere along the seam allowance of the patch, but do not sew through the patch yet.

4 Use the tip of the needle to turn under a bit of seam allowance at a time and then hold it in place while you sew it down. You can either use straight stitches, as with raw-edge appliqué, or you can use the slip stitch (page 26) to completely hide the stitching.

Basting

Basting is really handy for projects where you would otherwise have to use a lot of pins to hold everything together. Although there's nothing wrong with using pins, they can get in the way and are, of course, a finger-poking hazard. Basting is really straightforward: longish straight or running stitches that can be easily removed. It does take more time to baste things together but it is usually time well spent. Layers of fabric won't slip and move around, so the end result will look neater. Use regular sewing thread for basting, and use a color that you can easily see when it's time to remove it.

Trimming Seam Allowance

Seam allowance is a guideline to help us sew things in the correct size. But it also serves to protect the seam itself. If you sew too close to the edge of the fabric, it may start unravelling and the seam may come apart, too, if there's not enough fabric to hang onto.

But sometimes the seam allowance gets in the way, making seams and corners too bulky. This is especially the case when using several layers of fabric or when using fabrics that are somewhat inflexible. In those cases, it can be necessary to trim off some of the seam allowance after you have sewn the seam. Cut off half to a third of the seam allowance, depending on the type of fabric. If the fabric is loosely woven, you will need to leave more seam allowance.

CLIPPING AND NOTCHING

You should always clip corners and notch curves in the seam allowance of your projects. The reason for this is that the seam may look nice and flat on the wrong side, but when you turn it inside out, there is a lot less space for the fabric. In a turned corner, for example, the fabric gets bunched together in half the space. So you want to clip that corner. For all clipping and notching: be careful not to cut into the seam! You'll want to clip or notch in the following locations:

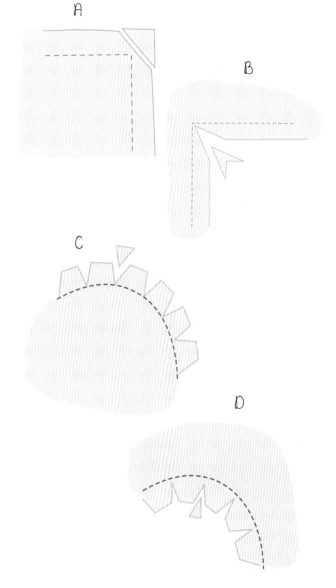

* Outer corner *(fig. A)*: Simply clip off the corner diagonally, and there should be plenty of room to make your corner nice and sharp.
* Inner corner *(fig. B)*: Cut a triangular notch into the corner.
* Convex curves *(fig. C)*: Cut triangular notches all along the curve. If you have pinking shears, they will do the job for you very quickly.
* Concave curves *(fig. D)*: Clip the edge as if you were cutting tabs.

Slip Stitch

This is sometimes called hidden stitch because it is hidden inside the fabric and is pretty much invisible. It can be used for sewing stuffing holes in softies or closing seams. It is also great for sewing binding on quilts or finishing turning gaps in bags.

To make the stitch invisible, use sewing thread in the same color as the fabric. You work the slip stitch from the right side of the piece, but all the stitching takes place on the wrong side. Take care not to sew the slip stitching too tightly or the seam will start to pucker.

1 Thread your needle and tie a knot at the end to hold it in place. Fold under the excess fabric along both sides of the opening; the folds are your seam line. Hold or pin the two folded edges together.

2 Insert the needle from the wrong side through one of the folded edges. Push the needle through to the right side. The knot should be on the wrong side of the fold.

3 Pull the needle and thread all the way through, and then insert the needle on the other folded edge, directly across from where it just exited. Slide the needle along the fold on the wrong side and the pull it out about ⅜ inch (1 cm) from where you inserted it. Insert the needle directly across on the other folded edge and repeat.

4 Continue this back and forth stitching until you have closed the opening. Make a couple of hidden stitches along the section that was already sewn together. This will make the seam more even.

5 Tie off the thread.

Knots

Whether you want to use knots or not in embroidery is a matter of choice. In some cases, knots can have a less than desirable effect, but they can also be quite practical. If the item you are stitching on will be used a lot or washed a lot, it may be a good idea to use knots to secure the stitches. But if the stitched project is only for decoration, it will probably be fine without any knots. If the back of the work will be visible then you may also wish to eliminate the knots.

MAKING A KNOT

If you do want to use knots, here's one way to make one very quickly and easily:

1 Thread the needle.

2 Holding the needle with the thumb and index finger of one hand, lay the tail of the thread along the needle so the tail extends just beyond the eye of the needle.

3 Hold on to both the needle and the thread tail with one hand, then twist the thread around the needle a couple of times with the other hand. Push the twists of thread toward the eye of the needle and then hold on to those along with the needle and the thread tail.

4 Grab the needle with the other hand and pull it away from the thread tail and the thread twists. Keep holding on to these while you pull the thread all the way through.

At the end you should have a knot. It may take a few tries to get this to work, but it is a great way to do a knot!

WASTE KNOT

A so-called waste knot is a great way to both use a knot and not use a knot. You have the benefit of the knot holding the thread in place at the start of your stitching, but at the end you can just cut it off—hence the name, because the knot is thrown away, wasted.

1 Cut your thread 2 inches (5 cm) longer than you would if using a regular knot. Make a knot at the end of your thread and then push the thread through from the front of the fabric, so the knot sits on the front.

2 Push the thread through on the opposite side of your stitch direction. If you stitch from left to right, the knot should be on the right, and on the left if you stitch from right to left. By doing this, you will be stitching across the length of thread coming from the knot, securing the thread.

3 Once you're done embroidering, secure the thread on the back and cut off the knot from the front plus any excess thread.

knot on front of fabric

SECURING THREAD ON THE BACK

You do not need to tie a knot to finish off a thread. It can be difficult to do this anyway, so you might as well avoid it completely. Once you've finished the last stitch, the needle should be on the back of the work. Weave the needle and thread end through some of the stitching. This will secure the thread. You can double back through the stitching for extra security. This will make for a far less bumpy back than if you try to knot the thread ends.

In some cases, it isn't possible to weave the thread end into other stitching—for example, if you've done a single stitch relatively far away from any other stitches. Then you will have to make do with the back of the stitch itself. With most stitches there will be at least a couple of tiny straight stitches on the back. You can use these to loop the thread through, and you can then weave the end through this loop. It will be a bit bumpier than simple weaving in, but sometimes that can't be helped. When you have a single stitch like this, the one thing you don't want to do is weave in

the end through that far away stitching, because that will mean stretches of thread on the back which may be visible through the fabric. It will also make the back look very messy.

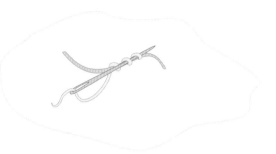

DISAPPEARING KNOT

It's not a magic trick, but you can make knots disappear! Some projects do not have a back, or the back isn't accessible. For example, when sewing shut the opening of a softie, there's no access to the wrong side where you would normally hide the knot. But you can make the knots disappear into the fabric.

1 When you have finished your stitching, push the needle up through the fabric about ½ inch (1.3 cm) from the last stitch.

2 Wind the thread around the tip of the needle, as if you were making a French knot (page 30). But instead of pushing the needle through the fabric, pull it through the thread to make a knot. The knot should be fairly close to the fabric.

3 Use the end of the needle to enlarge the hole in the fabric where you pushed the needle and thread through. It can be a bit tricky, but should be doable with most fabrics. Push the needle through the hole and then pull it back up about ⅝ inch (1.6 cm) from the hole, and pull the thread tight so the knot pops through the hole to the back of the fabric.

4 Cut off excess thread and the thread will sink into the fabric. With the tip of the needle, tease the hole back together. You may not be able to make it completely invisible at first, but with time the hole will disappear and the knot will be completely hidden.

Stitch Glossary

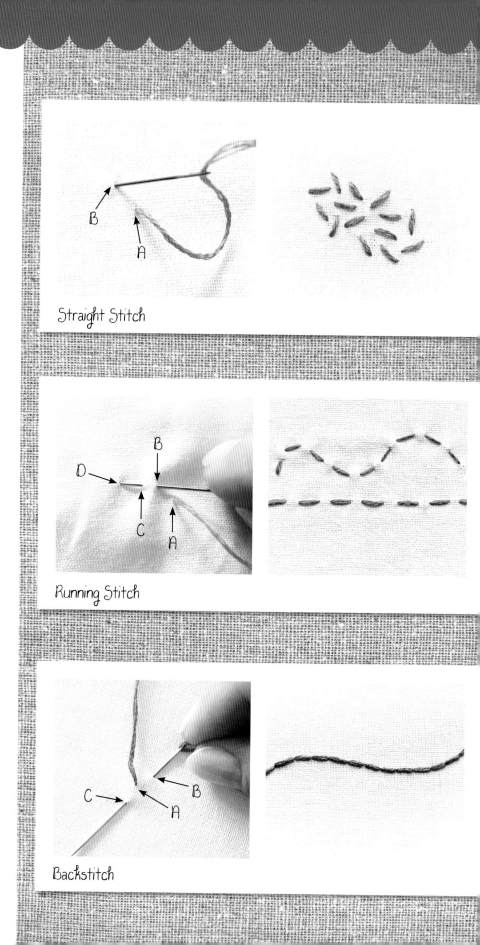

Straight Stitch

Running Stitch

Backstitch

Straight Stitch

Push the needle up through the fabric from the back at A, then back down again at B.

Running Stitch

Work in a similar fashion to straight stitch, but instead of single, scattered stitches, running stitches follow a line, whether straight or curved. Push the needle up through the fabric from the back at A, back down again at B, then up at C, down at D and so on.

Backstitch

This stitch is normally used as an outline stitch, and you start it in the same way you start a running stitch: Push the needle through the fabric at A, then back down at B. Push up at C, then down at A.

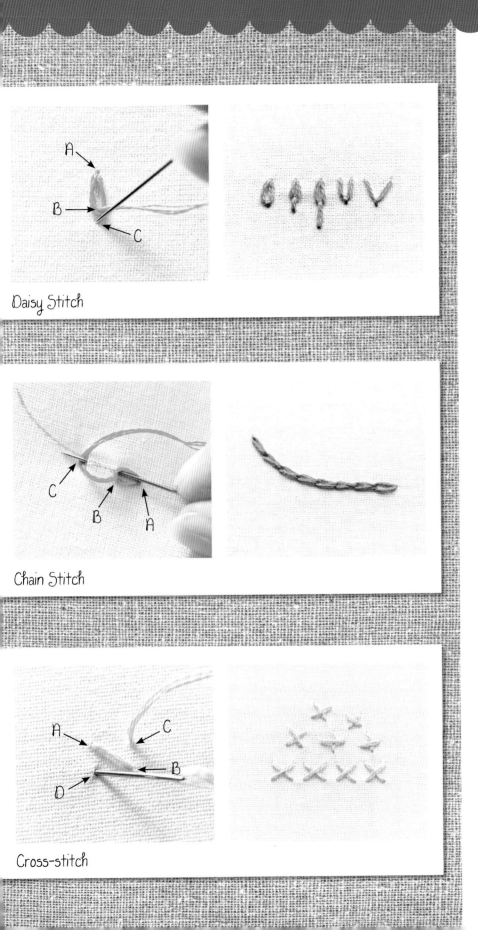

Daisy Stitch

Push the needle up at A, and grab it with your stitching hand. Hold on to the thread with the other hand (okay, maybe the whole hand is a bit much; a single finger should suffice) so the thread doesn't slip back through the fabric when you push the needle down again at A. Do not pull the thread all the way through; leave a small loop. Pull the thread up at B on the inside of the loop, then down at C to finish the stitch.

Chain Stitch

Chain stitch is worked like a daisy stitch, but, as the name suggests, it is a chain of stitches. Pull the needle through at A, and grab it with your stitching hand. Hold the thread with the thumb of your other hand and push the needle down again at A. Do not pull the thread all the way through; leave a small loop on the front of the fabric. Pull the needle up at B, then push it down again at B and up again at C, and you are ready to make the next link in the chain.

Cross-stitch

It is easiest to make an even cross-stitch on a loosely woven cloth. Count an even number of threads in the fabric for the width and the height, for example 4 x 4. Pull the needle up at A, down at B, up at C, and finally down at D.

Daisy Stitch

Chain Stitch

Cross-stitch

French Knot

The examples show knots made with 3 strands. The group on the left is wound three times, the one in the middle is wound twice, and the right one is wound once around the needle. To make this stitch, pull the needle through from the back of the fabric. Then, holding the needle in your stitching hand and the thread in the other, with the thread closest to you, wind the thread around the needle twice.

Keep holding on to both thread and needle so the thread is taut as you move the needle back to the fabric and push the needle back through the fabric. The point where you push the needle down should be about the distance from the entry hole as the width of the thread you are using. Wind the thread around the needle multiple times to create a larger knot.

French Knot

Satin Stitch

Satin Stitch

Mark the outline of the shape you wish to stitch on fabric. Either use a pen that can be washed out or make the outline with a backstitch (page 28), using a single strand of thread. Practice satin stitch on felt until you get familiar with it; it can become uneven on loosely woven fabric.

Starting in the middle of the shape, bring the needle up at A and down at B. The next stitch comes up at C and down at D, then back up again at E. Continue in this way, up on

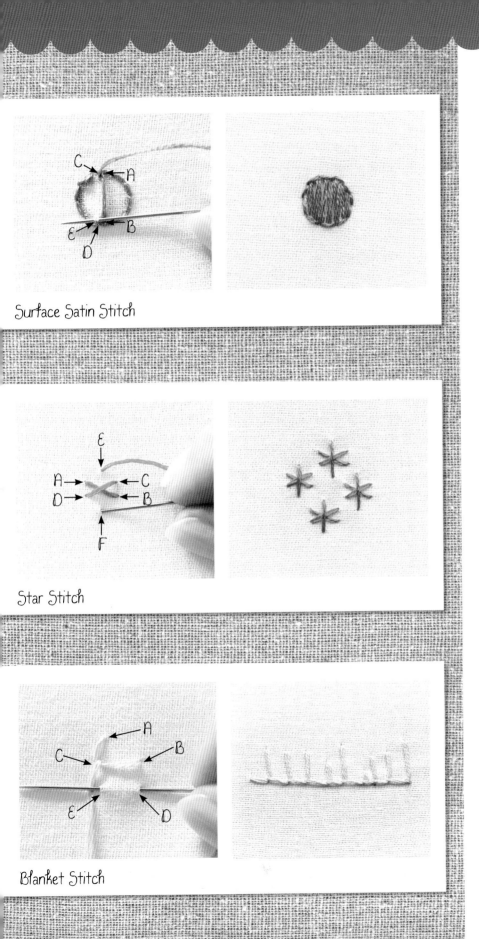

Surface Satin Stitch

Star Stitch

Blanket Stitch

one side, down on the opposite side, until you reach one end. Work the other half in the same way, starting in the middle of the shape.

You will see that there's an almost exactly mirrored shape on the back of the fabric. The stitches should be separated by one thread of the fabric to get the most even result. It is important not to pull the thread too tight, or the stitching will be uneven.

Surface Satin Stitch

This is similar to satin stitch, but is not as closely stitched. And unlike satin stitch, there is very little stitching on the underside of the fabric. Bring the needle up at A and push it down at B. Bring it up again at C, down at D, and up at E. Continue this alternating pattern to fill the whole shape.

Star Stitch

The star stitch is almost identical to cross-stitch, but the initial stitch should be wider than it is high. Pull the needle up at A, down at B, up at C, and down at D. Then pull the needle up at E and finally down at F.

Blanket Stitch

Push the needle up at A, down at B, and up again at C, catching the thread so it makes a reversed L shape. Continue along the design line: down at D, up at E, and so on.

Buttonhole Wheel Stitch

The buttonhole wheel stitch is basically worked in the same way as the blanket stitch, but it is worked around a circle. Pull the needle up at A, push it down at B and then up at C, catching the thread to make a "spoke" on the wheel. Push the needle down again at B and up at D to create the next spoke. When you get back to the beginning, finish the wheel with a tiny straight stitch.

Maidenhair

To achieve an evenly straight spine with this stitch, it is best worked on a central guideline. Pull up the needle at A, push it down at B, and up at C, making sure to catch the thread to create a V shape. Down at D and up at E. Down at F and up at G. Make a similar group, but mirrored, on the other side of the spine and continue alternating groups on each side. The bottom of one group should line up with the top of the group below.

You can vary the length of the stitches to create different effects. You can also add more Vs to each group. Just bear in mind that the more you add, the larger the stitches will become, and long stitches will not stay completely straight.

Petal Stitch

This stitch is ideal for curved lines, but can be a bit tricky on a concave curve where the stitches might become a bit squished together. Start by making a short straight

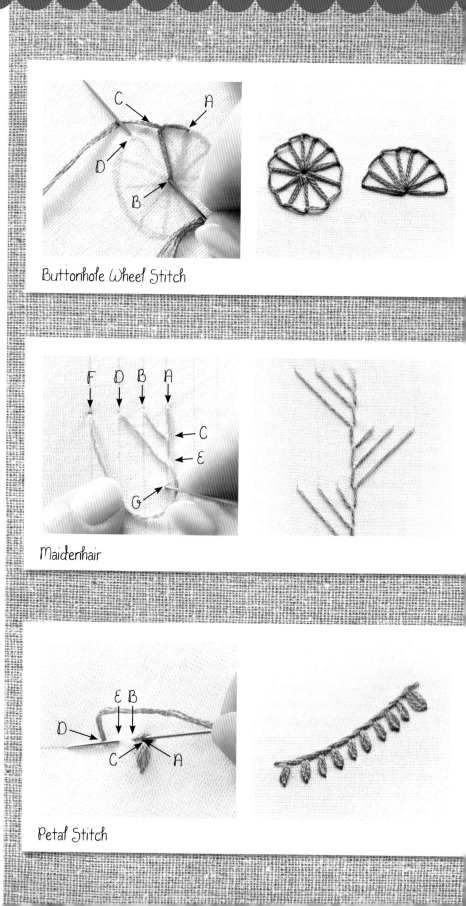

Buttonhole Wheel Stitch

Maidenhair

Petal Stitch

Whipped Backstitch

Fern Stitch

Pointe Russe

stitch (A-B). Then pull the needle up at C and make a daisy stitch (page 29) at a slight angle to the straight stitch. Pull the needle up at D and push it down at C. Pull it up at E and make a Daisy stitch as before. Continue this way along your line to be stitched. You should always bring the needle up on the side of the straight stitch that is closest to you.

Whipped Backstitch

This technique can also be used for other outline stitches, such as chain stitch or running stitch.

Bring the needle up at A, at one end of the backstitch, then weave (or whip) the contrasting thread around the underlying stitches. The whipped thread is not stitched onto the fabric, apart from the start and finish of the line. At the end, finish by pushing the needle and thread through the fabric on the opposite side of the line of backstitch.

Fern Stitch

Bring the needle up at A, down at B, up at C, down at A, then up at D. Then bring it down again at A and up at E to start the next group of three stitches.

This stitch follows a curve very well. A guideline may be necessary to achieve an even look.

Pointe Russe

To sew this fan-shaped stitch, make a straight stitch in the middle and then make two angled stitches on either side of it, starting with the smallest stitches.

pomegranate parade skirt

The pomegranate-inspired design on this little girl's skirt would look right at home on grown-up attire, too! (Coordinating mother-daughter outfits, anyone?)

you will need

* Motif (page 36)
* Skirt
* Rickrack, ½ inch (1.3 cm) wide; match the length to the circumference of your skirt

* Embroidery floss, 1 skein each: orange red, dark red, light green, kelly green, light turquoise, medium blue

I used DMC embroidery floss colors 606, 321, 907, 911, 3846, and 3843.

instructions

STITCH THE EMBROIDERY

1 Enlarge the motif to your liking. Transfer the motif to the skirt using the method that best fits the fabric.

2 Stitch the motif.

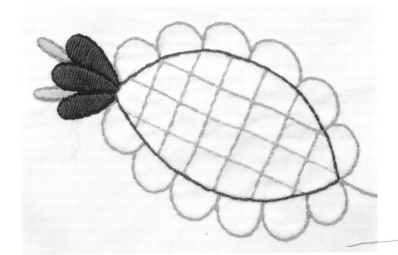

ADD THE RICKRACK EMBELLISHMENT

3 Measure the circumference of the skirt hem. Cut rickrack to this length + 1 inch (2.5 cm).

4 Pin the rickrack on the wrong side of the skirt along the hemline, with approximately half of it showing below the hem. Overlap the ends by ¼ inch (6 mm) and cut off any excess rickrack.

5 Topstitch along the hem to attach the rickrack.

placement on skirt

motif

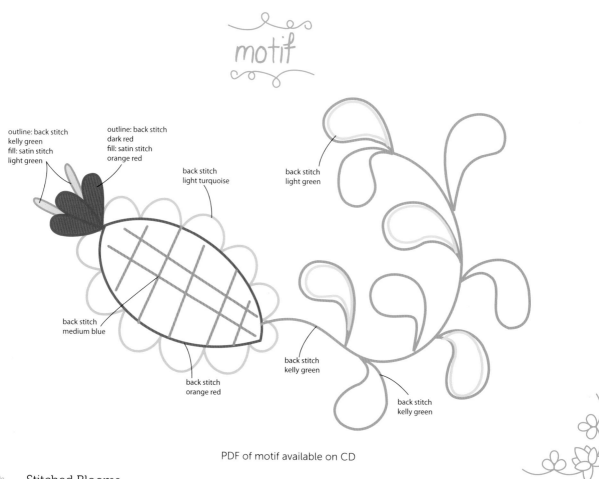

outline: back stitch
kelly green
fill: satin stitch
light green

outline: back stitch
dark red
fill: satin stitch
orange red

back stitch
light turquoise

back stitch
light green

back stitch
medium blue

back stitch
orange red

back stitch
kelly green

back stitch
kelly green

PDF of motif available on CD

holiday hoops

Stitch up these winter ornaments in no time, then hang them in your home (or cubicle!), and you'll feel joyous all season long.

you will need

* Motifs (page 39)
* 4 pieces of red faux leather, each 8 inches (20.3 cm) square
* Four 4-inch (10.2 cm) wooden embroidery hoops

* White acrylic paint (optional)
* Glue that will adhere the faux leather and hoops (a glue stick will not do!)
* Red gingham ribbon, ⅜ inch (1 cm) wide

* Embroidery floss: 1 skein of white

I used DMC embroidery floss color blanc.

instructions

1 Enlarge the motifs by 150 percent. Center each motif in a leather square, and transfer it using the transfer paper method (page 18).

2 Stitch the motifs.

3 Wash or rub off any transfer lines.

4 Paint the outer hoop rings (the ones with the screw) if you like. There's no need to paint the inner hoops because they won't be seen.

5 Hoop the pieces with the motifs in the middle. Leave them like this for an hour or so. This will slightly shape the faux leather, creating a guide for where to apply glue.

6 Remove the fabric from the hoops and apply glue to the back side of the shaped faux leather. Don't use too much, or it may seep through and stain the front. Follow the application instructions for the particular type of glue you are using, and apply it in a well-ventilated area if the glue is solvent-based.

7 Place the faux leather over the unpainted hoop ring, and then place the painted ring on top of the faux leather. Adjust if necessary, and tighten the screw. Depending on the glue you've used, you may have to do this step quickly to adjust the leather. Allow the glue to dry properly.

8 Cut off excess faux leather so the hoops will hang flush on the wall.

9 Attach the ribbon.

motifs

enlarge 150%

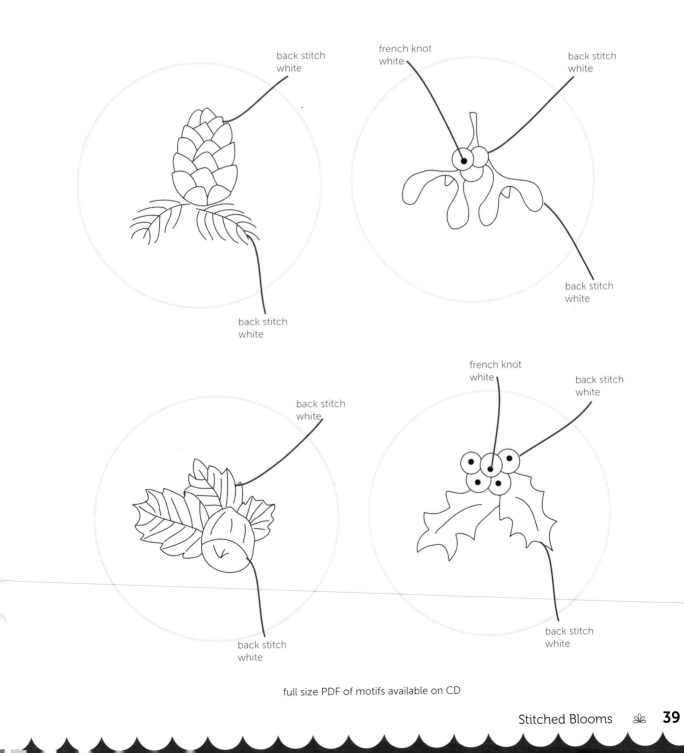

back stitch
white

french knot
white

back stitch
white

back stitch
white

back stitch
white

back stitch
white

back stitch
white

french knot
white

back stitch
white

back stitch
white

back stitch
white

full size PDF of motifs available on CD

pretty organized calendar

Keep everything running right on schedule with this calendar—or use it as a photo frame!

✿✿✿✿✿✿✿✿✿✿✿✿✿✿✿✿✿✿✿✿✿✿✿✿✿✿✿✿✿✿✿✿✿✿✿✿

you will need

* Motif and Template (page 43)
* ¾ yard (.7 m) of fabric
* Clear vinyl fabric, 8¾ x 9½ inches (22.2 x 24.1 cm)
* Interfacing, 2 pieces, each 9½ inches (24.1 cm) square
* Double-sided tape

* Calendar insert (page 126)
* 1 bamboo dowel, 12 inches (30.5 cm) long, ¼ inch (.6 cm) in diameter
* Embroidery floss, 1 skein each: orange, spring green, lilac, purple, medium yellow, light yellow, orange red, bright red, dark bubblegum pink, light spring green

I used DMC embroidery floss colors 741, 906, 209, 3837, 972, 307, 606, 666, 956, and 3819.

✿✿✿✿✿✿✿✿✿✿✿✿✿✿✿✿✿✿✿✿✿✿✿✿✿✿✿✿✿✿✿✿✿✿✿✿

instructions

CUT THE FABRIC

1 Cut the following pieces from fabric:
* 4 pieces, 9½ inches (24.1 cm) square, for the front and back panels
* 2 pieces, 3 x 1½ inches (7.6 x 3.8 cm), for hanging loops

STITCH THE EMBROIDERY

2 Enlarge the motif template by 275 percent. Center it on one of the fabric squares with an even amount of fabric on all sides. Transfer the motif.

3 Stitch the motif. Rinse off any transfer lines, if necessary, and iron the piece on the back.

4 Apply interfacing to the back of the piece and on one other fabric square, following manufacturer's directions.

MAKE THE HANGING LOOPS

5 Press under the long sides ¼ inch (6 mm). Then fold the strip down the middle, press, and pin.

6 Topstitch on both long sides of the narrow strip.

7 Repeat for the other loop.

MAKE THE FRONT PANEL

8 On the stitched square, mark a ¼-inch (6 mm) seam allowance from the edge of the fabric on all sides. Also mark a 4-inch (10.2 cm) turning gap in the center of what will be the bottom edge. Lay this square on top of another fabric square with right sides facing each other.

9 Fold the hanging loops in half and place them between the two fabric layers on the top edge, aligning raw edges, ⅜ inch (1 cm) from the embroidered running stitch on each side.

10 Stitch the layers together. Trim off excess seam allowance and clip the corners. Turn right side out and push corners into shape. Slip stitch the turning gap closed.

MAKE THE OPENING

11 On the stitched side of the calendar front, use a water-soluble pen to mark a line ¼ inch (6 mm) from the inside running stitch on all sides. Mark another line 1 inch (2.5 cm) from the running stitch line. In the corners, draw a diagonal line between the two squares you just drew.

12 Cut out the smaller square and clip along the diagonal corner lines.

13 Use the opening and clipped corners as a guide to draw the same lines on the back of the piece. Cut it out in the same way.

14 Fold under the raw edges along the first drawn line, in the front and the back. Pin in place. Make sure that the folded edges on the front and back line up. Topstitch as close to the fold as possible. It may be easier to topstitch if you baste the layers together first and then remove the pins.

15 Gently rinse out the lines you marked.

MAKE THE BACK PIECE

16 Layer the fabric and vinyl pieces like so: fabric, vinyl, fabric. The vinyl piece is shorter than the two pieces of fabric, to create a pocket, so make sure to line the three pieces up at the bottom edge. Mark the turning gap at the bottom edge. Mark the seam allowance at ⅜ inch (1 cm) from the fabric edge if necessary.

17 Stitch the three layers together. Cut off excess seam allowance and clip the corners. Turn right side out and push the corners into shape. Slip stitch the turning gap.

SEW THE SECTIONS TOGETHER

18 Pin the front and back sewn squares together, with the vinyl side of the back piece facing the wrong side of the front piece. Starting at the top right corner and ending at the top left corner, slipstitch the two sections together, only stitching through the two outermost layers. Don't pull the stitching too tight or the fabric will pucker at the edge. You can also topstitch the sections together with the sewing machine, but because there are quite a few layers to sew through, it may be difficult to get an even result.

19 Cut 4 pieces of double-sided tape, and tape the frame to the clear vinyl. This will stop the opening from gaping.

20 Print and cut out the calendar insert and insert in the pocket. Place the bamboo dowel in the loops and hang on a nail or hook.

template & motif

enlarge 275%

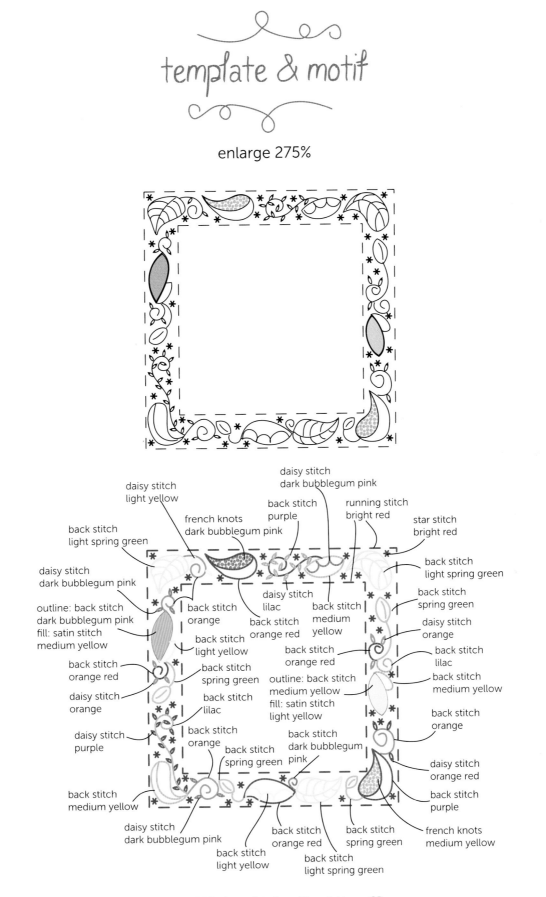

daisy stitch
light yellow

daisy stitch
dark bubblegum pink

back stitch
purple

running stitch
bright red

french knots
dark bubblegum pink

star stitch
bright red

back stitch
light spring green

back stitch
light spring green

daisy stitch
dark bubblegum pink

back stitch
spring green

outline: back stitch
dark bubblegum pink
fill: satin stitch
medium yellow

back stitch
orange

daisy stitch
lilac

back stitch
medium yellow

daisy stitch
orange

back stitch
orange red

back stitch
light yellow

back stitch
orange red

back stitch
lilac

back stitch
orange red

back stitch
orange red

daisy stitch
orange

outline: back stitch
medium yellow
fill: satin stitch
light yellow

back stitch
medium yellow

back stitch
spring green

back stitch
orange

daisy stitch
purple

back stitch
lilac

back stitch
dark bubblegum
pink

daisy stitch
orange red

back stitch
orange

back stitch
spring green

back stitch
purple

back stitch
medium yellow

back stitch
spring green

french knots
medium yellow

daisy stitch
dark bubblegum pink

back stitch
orange red

back stitch
spring green

back stitch
light yellow

back stitch
light spring green

scandinavian snö mittens

Mittens remind me of building igloos and snowmen in my grandparents' backyard. Adding a floral pattern makes them the perfect winter accessory.

you will need

* Motifs (page 46)
* A pair of mittens

* 2-ply crewel wool, 1 skein each: egg yolk yellow, bubblegum pink, purple, kelly green, yellow green

I used Appleton's crewel wool colors 555, 944, 453, 425, and 253.

instructions

1 Enlarge the motifs to your liking. Center the motifs on the backs of the mittens, and transfer them. Choose a transfer method that is best suited to the material of the mittens. (The mittens in the example are a wool mix, and I found that the tissue paper method works best for this.)

2 Stitch the motifs.

3 Gently tear away the tissue paper.

before or after?

* If you make the mittens yourself, it's easiest to stitch the motifs before sewing the mittens together.
* If embroidering mittens that are already sewn together, you may want to insert something stiff inside to help avoid stitching all the way through the mitten. A sturdy piece of cardstock would do.

motifs

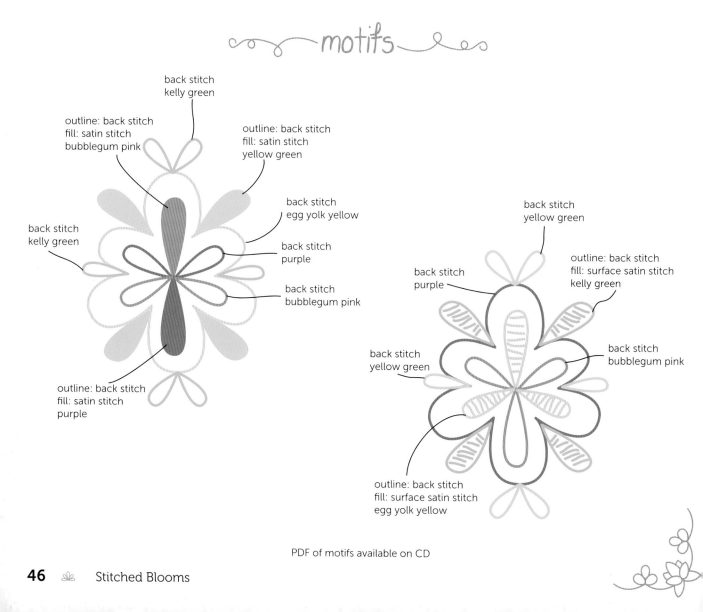

back stitch kelly green

outline: back stitch
fill: satin stitch
bubblegum pink

outline: back stitch
fill: satin stitch
yellow green

back stitch
egg yolk yellow

back stitch
purple

back stitch
bubblegum pink

back stitch
kelly green

outline: back stitch
fill: satin stitch
purple

back stitch
yellow green

outline: back stitch
fill: surface satin stitch
kelly green

back stitch
purple

back stitch
bubblegum pink

back stitch
yellow green

outline: back stitch
fill: surface satin stitch
egg yolk yellow

PDF of motifs available on CD

pom-pom luminaries

These candle bags are quick to make, and pom-pom fringe adds extra fun! Whip up a set in a weekend and set them out at your next casual dinner party.

you will need

* Motifs (page 49)
* White fabric, 9¼ x 6 inches (23.5 x 15.2 cm) per bag
* Interfacing (optional, see Fabric Notes)
* Mini pom-pom trim in pink, light green, and white, 6 inches (15.2 cm) per bag

* Small glass or jar
* Votive candle for each bag
* Embroidery floss, 1 skein each: yellow, spring green, darkish pink, orange, light turquoise

I used DMC embroidery floss colors 307, 907, 602, 970, and 3846.

fabric notes

* The fabric dimensions include a ¼-inch (6 mm) seam allowance.
* If your fabric of choice is soft, you might want to use interfacing cut to the same size as the fabric.

instructions

1 Fold the fabric in half. Mark 1½ inches (3.8 cm) from the fold; this is the bottom line of the motif. Unfold the fabric.

2 Center a motif on one half of the fabric, and transfer it.

3 Stitch the motif.

4 Rinse off any transfer lines.

5 Apply interfacing if necessary, following manufacturer's directions.

6 Fold the fabric with right sides facing. Stitch together along the sides, then stitch diagonally across each corner, 1 inch (2.5 cm) from the pointed edge, to "box" the corner. This will help the bag stand up. Clip the seam allowance at both corners.

7 Turn the bag right side out. Press a ¼-inch (6 mm) double-fold hem along the top raw edge of the bag, and topstitch.

8 Stitch one of the pom-pom trims along the top edge.

9 To use the bag, place a small jar inside, with the candle inside the jar. Never place a lit candle in the bag itself; always use a jar that is the same height as the bag. Do not leave unattended when lit.

motifs

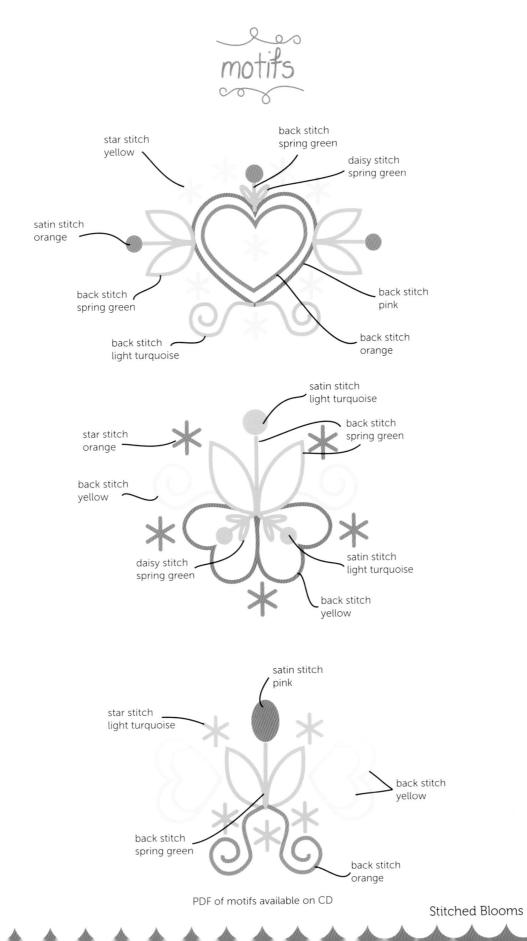

star stitch
yellow

back stitch
spring green

daisy stitch
spring green

satin stitch
orange

back stitch
spring green

back stitch
pink

back stitch
light turquoise

back stitch
orange

satin stitch
light turquoise

star stitch
orange

back stitch
spring green

back stitch
yellow

daisy stitch
spring green

satin stitch
light turquoise

back stitch
yellow

satin stitch
pink

star stitch
light turquoise

back stitch
yellow

back stitch
spring green

back stitch
orange

PDF of motifs available on CD

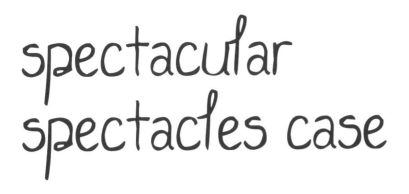

spectacular spectacles case

Keep your glasses and shades scratch free by storing them in this lovely little case. Adding a microfiber lining keeps dust at bay, too!

❀❀❀❀❀❀❀❀❀❀❀❀❀❀❀❀❀❀❀❀❀❀❀❀❀❀❀❀

you will need

* Motif (page 52)
* Template (page 53)
* Felt, light turquoise, 8 inches (20.3 cm) square
* Fabric for lining, 8 inches (20.3 cm) square

* Fusible interfacing, 8 inches (20.3 cm) square
* Tissue paper, 5 inches (12.7 cm) square
* Embroidery floss, 1 skein each: light turquoise, dark turquoise, dark blue

I used DMC embroidery floss colors 3846, 3844, and 3765.

❀❀❀❀❀❀❀❀❀❀❀❀❀❀❀❀❀❀❀❀❀❀❀❀❀❀❀❀

instructions

1 Enlarge the template by 150 percent. Using the template, cut the following. A ¼-inch (6 mm) seam allowance is included in the template.
* 1 piece from felt
* 1 piece from lining fabric
* 1 piece from interfacing, using the lining fabric template

2 Apply the interfacing to the wrong side of the fabric, following the manufacturer's directions.

3 Transfer the motif to tissue paper, and baste the paper in place on the right side of the exterior/felt piece.

4 Stitch the motif, and then gently tear away the tissue paper.

5 Fold the exterior piece in half as indicated on the template, with right sides facing each other. Sew together along the bottom and the side.

6 Repeat for the lining piece, but leave open the turning gap as shown on the template.

7 Clip the corners and cut off excess seam allowance on both pieces. Do not cut off seam allowance at the turning gap. It will be easier to sew the gap together later if the seam allowance is still there.

8 Turn the exterior piece right side out and place it inside the lining piece. Line up the top edges and the side seam, and pin the two cases together.

9 Starting at the end of the seams from steps 5 and 6, sew along the diagonal side. Then sew a continuous seam around the top of the case and down the short side. Stop just before the side seam from steps 5 and 6. Trim off excess seam allowance and notch the corners.

10 Pull the case through the turning gap and push out the corners of the exterior piece.

11 Topstich or slip stich the turning gap together, and push the lining piece inside the exterior piece.

motif

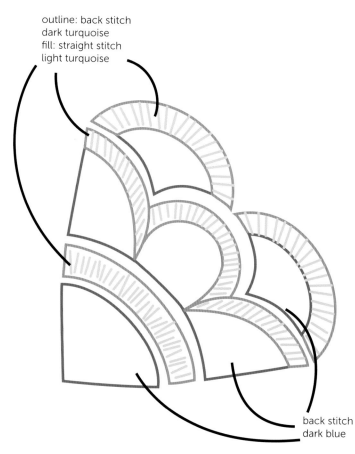

outline: back stitch
dark turquoise
fill: straight stitch
light turquoise

back stitch
dark blue

PDF of motif available on CD

template

enlarge 150%

cut 1 from felt
cut 1 from fabric
cut 1 from interfacing

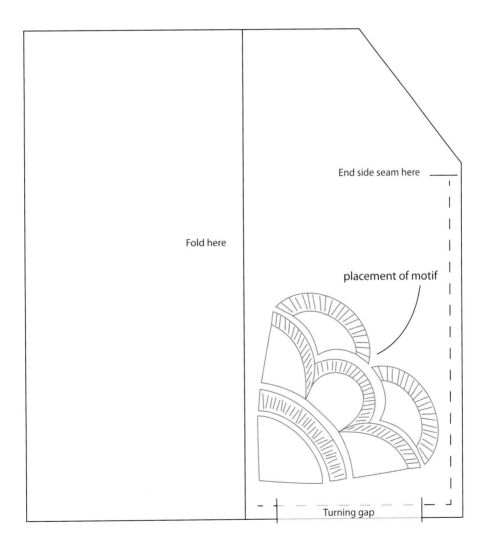

Fold here

End side seam here

placement of motif

Turning gap

full size PDF of template available on CD

botanical art

Embroidery is a wonderful way to keep connections with the places you love. These illustrations of a Daisy, a Rosa Canina, and a Hibiscus celebrate places very dear to me—Denmark, England, and Hawaii.

you will need

* Motifs (page 55)
* 3 pieces of white fabric, each 6¾ x 8¾ inches (17.2 x 22.2 cm)
* Iron-on interfacing, 3 pieces the same size as the fabric (optional)

* 3 picture frames, with mounting mats 5 x 7 inches (12.7 x 17.8 cm)
* Acid-free tape or masking tape
* Embroidery floss: 1 skein of black

I used DMC embroidery floss color 310.

instructions

1 Enlarge the motifs by 150 percent, and transfer each to one of the three fabric pieces. Stitch them with only 2 strands so the stitched lines do not become too thick. When done, make sure to cut off any thread ends so they won't show through the fabric.

2 Apply the iron-on interfacing following manufacturer's directions. This is optional, but it will make the fabric a bit easier to handle.

3 Cut the fabric pieces to size, taking care to cut them about ½ inch (1.3 cm) smaller than the mounting mat on all four sides.

4 Center the mounting mat from the frame on the stitched piece.

5 Mount the stitched piece on the inside of the mounting mat with acid-free tape.

motifs

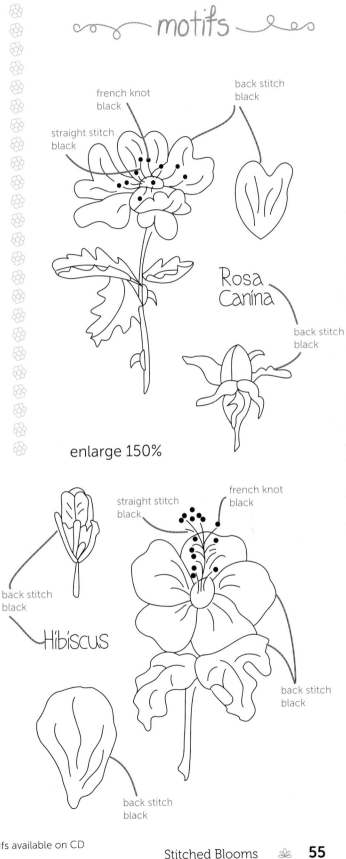

french knot
black

back stitch
black

straight stitch
black

Rosa
Canina

back stitch
black

enlarge 150%

back stitch
black

french knot
black

Bellis
Perennis

back stitch
black

straight stitch
black

french knot
black

back stitch
black

Hibiscus

back stitch
black

back stitch
black

full size PDF of motifs available on CD

blomma bag

From a distance you can see bright pops of color, but look closer and there's a joyful little flower! Stitch this on any bag that needs a bit of pep—a plain tote works wonderfully.

you will need

* Motif (page 57)
* Tote bag
* Felt, a 6-inch (15.2 cm) square of each color: pale yellow, light yellow, light blue, light turquoise, light pink, bubblegum pink, darkish pink, pale green, pale spring green, light mint
* Embroidery floss, 1 skein each (use colors that match the felt shapes): pale yellow, light yellow, light blue, light turquoise, light pink, bubblegum pink, darkish pink, pale spring green, light mint, dark green

I used DMC embroidery floss colors 3078, 445, 747, 3761, 963, 957, 602, 772, 966, and 701.

instructions

1 If you use the Belted Tote Bag pattern (see Tote Tips below), enlarge the motif by 300 percent. Otherwise, enlarge to your liking.

2 Transfer the motif to the bag, and pin the felt shapes in place. Appliqué the felt shapes using the buttonhole wheel stitch.

3 Stitch the rest of the motif in backstitch.

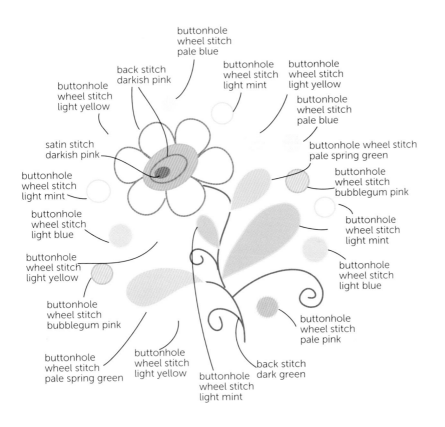

buttonhole wheel stitch pale blue

back stitch darkish pink

buttonhole wheel stitch light yellow

buttonhole wheel stitch light mint

buttonhole wheel stitch light yellow

buttonhole wheel stitch pale blue

satin stitch darkish pink

buttonhole wheel stitch pale spring green

buttonhole wheel stitch light mint

buttonhole wheel stitch bubblegum pink

buttonhole wheel stitch light blue

buttonhole wheel stitch light mint

buttonhole wheel stitch light yellow

buttonhole wheel stitch light blue

buttonhole wheel stitch bubblegum pink

buttonhole wheel stitch pale spring green

buttonhole wheel stitch light yellow

buttonhole wheel stitch light mint

back stitch dark green

buttonhole wheel stitch pale pink

tote tips

* If you're making a bag from scratch, it's easiest to stitch the motif before sewing the bag together. Make sure to resize the motif if necessary so it won't be obscured by any pleats or closures on the bag.
* The bag in this example was made using the Belted Tote Bag pattern from Michelle's Patterns (michellepatterns.com).

PDF of motif available on CD

obi belt

Paired with jeans or a long skirt, this too-cool
obi belt has just the right amount of floral flair.
Simple redwork flowers really pop against
the faux leather background.

you will need

* Template and motif (page 61)
* Faux leather, 29 x 8 inches
  (73.7 x 20.3 cm)
* Fabric, same size as the
  faux leather

* Velvet ribbon, 2 pieces, each
  43 inches (109.2 cm) long
* Embroidery floss, 1 skein
  each: bright red, medium red,
  burgundy
* Turning tool

*I used DMC embroidery floss
colors 666, 321, and 816.*

instructions

STITCH THE EMBROIDERY

1 Enlarge the belt template by 225 percent
and motif by 200 percent. Cut one each of the
faux leather and the fabric; cut on the fold as
indicated on the template. The template includes
a ¼-inch (6 mm) seam allowance.

2 Transfer the motif to the leather piece,
positioning it to one side (as marked on the
template) or centered in the front, as you like.
Place it just below the horizontal middle.

3 Stitch the motif. Wash or rub off any transfer
lines, if necessary.

MAKE THE BELT

4 If the ribbon you're using is likely to fray, make a narrow single-fold hem at one end.

5 Layer the elements as follows:
* Leather piece, right side facing up
* Ribbons, aligning and pinning the raw ends as indicated on the template (if the ribbon has a right side, this must face down)
* Lining piece, right side facing down

6 With the ribbon tucked between the fabrics away from the seam lines, stitch the belt together, leaving an opening on the bottom edge for turning, as shown on the pattern. Stitch back and forth across the ribbon's raw ends a couple of times to secure them.

7 Trim off excess seam allowance and notch all the way around the belt. If you've got pinking shears, this is what they're made for!

8 Turn belt right side out and push out the edges with a pointy object or turning tool. Slip stitch the opening closed.

9 Topstitch all the way around the edges, by hand or machine. It may be helpful to pin the edges so they lie flat. If using a machine, you may want to use a fairly large stitch and a needle suited to stitch through the leather. Check your sewing machine manual for the best settings.

template & motif

enlarge 200%

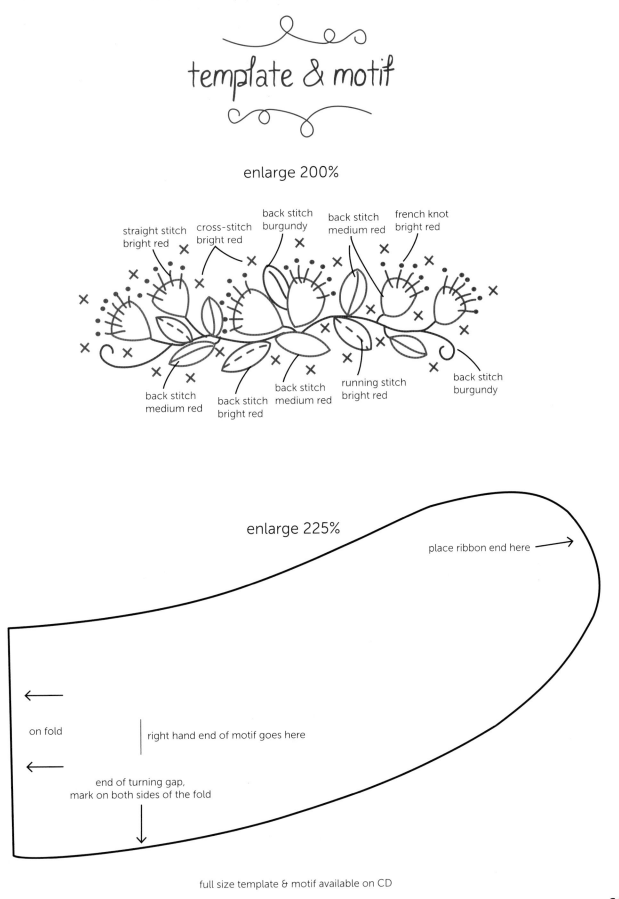

straight stitch
bright red

cross-stitch
bright red

back stitch
burgundy

back stitch
medium red

french knot
bright red

back stitch
medium red

back stitch
bright red

back stitch
medium red

running stitch
bright red

back stitch
burgundy

enlarge 225%

place ribbon end here →

← on fold

right hand end of motif goes here

← end of turning gap,
mark on both sides of the fold

full size template & motif available on CD

dala horse

The Dala horse is a much-loved symbol in Sweden.
I call this horse Gustav, after a 16th century Swedish king!

you will need

* Motif (page 65)
* Template (page 66)
* 2 pieces of blue felt,
  12 x 17 inches (30.5 x 43.2 cm)
* 2 pieces of light blue felt,
  4 x 4½ inches (10.2 x 11.4 cm)
* 2 pieces of tissue paper,
  12 x 17 inches (30.5 x 43.2 cm)
* 2 pieces of tissue paper,
  4 x 4½ inches (10.2 x 11.4 cm)
* Sewing thread in a color
  contrasting the blue felt,
  for basting

* Sewing thread in a color
  matching the blue felt
* Pointed tool such as a pencil
  or a crochet hook
* Embroidery hoop, 7 inches
  (optional)
* Fiberfill, polyester, or natural
  fiber as you prefer
* Embroidery floss, 1 skein
  each: medium turquoise,
  dark turquoise, medium
  blue, dark blue, blueish
  green, neon green

*I used DMC embroidery floss
colors 3846, 3844, 3843, 312,
3812, and E990.*

tip

Often fiberfill comes in
fairly large bags. If that is
more than you'll need, use
the stuffing from a cheap
pillow to stuff your softie.

instructions

1 Enlarge the horse template and motif by 200 percent. Reverse for one of the sides.

2 Transfer the template and pattern, including the outline of the horse, to one piece of tissue paper. Repeat for the reversed side.

3 Baste each tissue paper pattern in the center of a large piece of felt. Stitch a line of running stitches all along the outline of the horse on both pieces – this will show you where to sew the horse together later on.

4 Do not cut the horse pieces out of the felt rectangles yet. It will be a lot easier to stitch a nice regular shape of felt instead of dealing with limbs flopping all over the place.

5 Embroider the horse pieces. Then carefully remove the tissue paper and the basting stitches, but do not remove the line of running stitches.

6 Trace and cut out the saddle piece. You do not need a seam allowance for the saddle piece.

7 Transfer the saddle motif to tissue paper and baste in place on the felt. If you are embroidering on both sides of the horse, remember to reverse the saddle template and motif for one side.

8 Embroider the motifs on the saddle pieces first and then remove the tissue paper. Appliqué the saddle pieces to the horse pieces, making sure to leave the saddle tabs sticking out.

9 Cut the horse pieces from their rectangles, leaving a ¼ inch (6 mm) seam allowance all the way around the outside line. Take care not to cut into the saddle tabs.

10 Pin the two horse pieces together with the stitched right sides facing each other. Mark the turning gap along the horse's back. Sew the pieces together along the line of running stitches, leaving open the turning gap. Remove the running stitches.

11 Carefully notch around the curves of the horse and clip the corners. Space the notches about ¼ to ⅜ inch (6 mm to 1 cm) apart.

You can also carefully trim off excess seam allowance; this will make the seam smoother.

12 Turn the horse inside out through the turning gap and gently push the seam and corners into shape.

13 Stuff the horse. Start with the ear, mouth, and legs. Stuff them firmly to fill out the corners. Use the eraser end of a pencil to do this (don't use the lead end or it might poke through the felt).

14 Once the horse is stuffed, fold in the edges of the turning gap on the horse, and tuck the saddle tabs into the turning gap. Slip stitch together.

15 Add a decorative row of cross-stitches along the slip stitched seam. This will also give the seam extra strength.

> ### tip
>
> You don't need to use a hoop when stitching on felt, but since the horse is quite large, it may be easier to use a hoop to make the felt more rigid.

motif

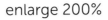

enlarge 200%

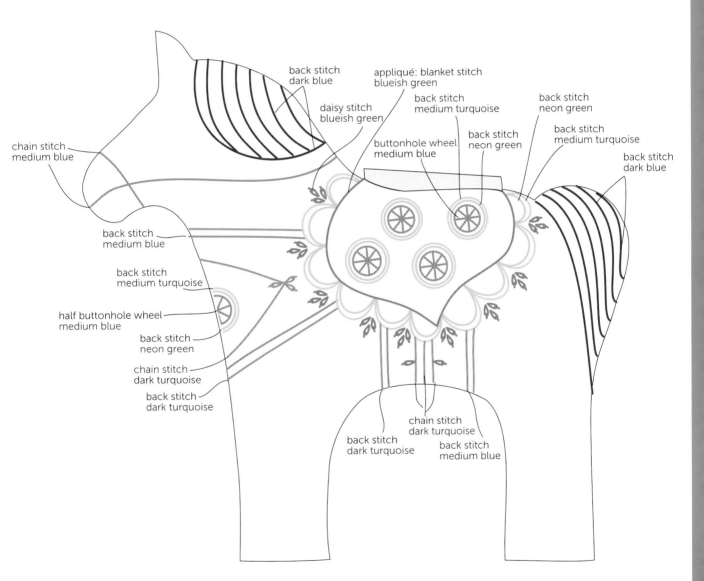

chain stitch
medium blue

back stitch
dark blue

daisy stitch
blueish green

appliqué: blanket stitch
blueish green

back stitch
medium turquoise

buttonhole wheel
medium blue

back stitch
neon green

back stitch
neon green

back stitch
medium turquoise

back stitch
dark blue

back stitch
medium blue

back stitch
medium turquoise

half buttonhole wheel
medium blue

back stitch
neon green

chain stitch
dark turquoise

back stitch
dark turquoise

chain stitch
dark turquoise

back stitch
dark turquoise

back stitch
medium blue

full size PDF of motif available on CD

templates

enlarge 200%

saddle tab

Saddle
cut 2 from felt

turning gap

seam allowance

Horse Softie
cut 2 from felt

place saddle here

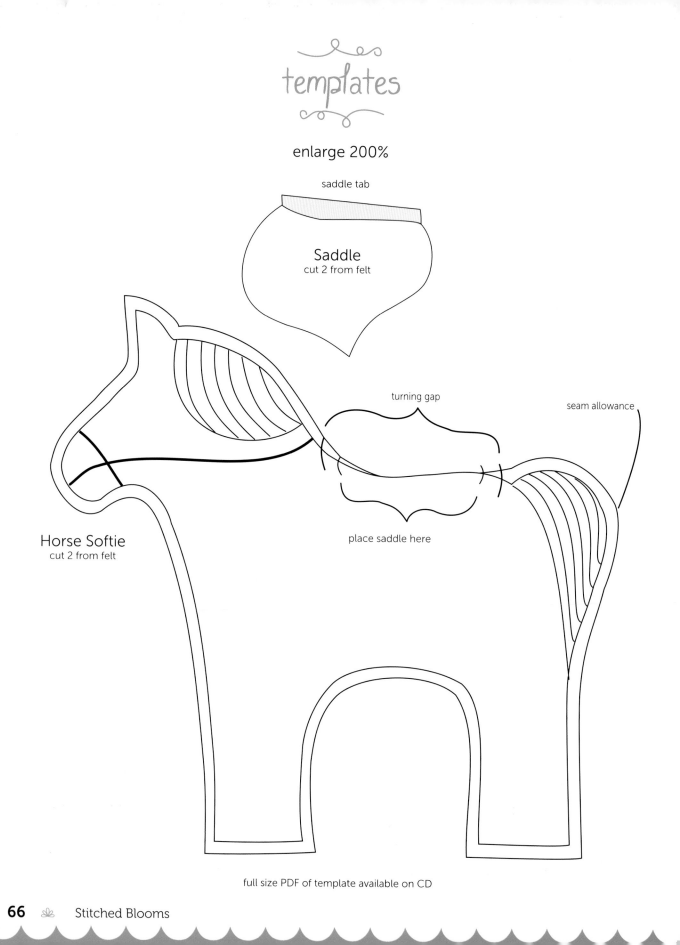

full size PDF of template available on CD

kit and kaboodle sewing kit

A pocket for floss and scissors, a needlebook for needles, and even a pincushion—this compact embroidery kit has everything you need when stitching on the go. Slip it into your handbag and you'll never be without your tools!

you will need

* Motif (page 69)
* Templates (pages 69 and 71)
* Lilac felt, 19 x 5 inches (48.3 x 12.7 cm)
* Fabric, 19 x 15 inches (48.3 x 38.1 cm)
* 40 inches (101.6 cm) of

orange double-fold bias tape or ribbon, ¾ inch (1.9 cm)
* Wool stuffing
* Interfacing (optional), same amount as the fabric
* 4 inches (10.2 cm) of hook-and-loop tape, ¾ inches (1.9 cm) wide

* Embroidery floss, 1 skein each: light orange, dark orange, orange red, purple

I used DMC embroidery floss colors 741, 970, 606, and 208.

instructions

CUT OUT THE PIECES

1 Enlarge templates by 225 percent. All pattern pieces, except for the felt leaves and felt pages, include a ¼-inch (6 mm) seam allowance.

2 Use the pattern pieces to cut out the following pieces from felt:
* 1 kit exterior
* 2-leaf appliqué for needlebook
* 1 piece for needlebook pages

3 Use the pattern pieces to cut out the following pieces from fabric:
* 1 kit interior
* 2 needlebook exterior pieces
* 1 pocket piece
* 2 pincushion pieces

MAKE THE PINCUSHION

4 Stitch a soft strip of hook-and-loop tape on the right side of one pincushion piece. Save the matching "catchy" strip for the kit interior.

5 Pin the two pincusion pieces together, right sides facing, and stitch, leaving the turning gap open as marked. Make sure to stop at the corners to pivot the fabric; this will give a sharper/crisper result.

6 Clip the corners and notch the curves of the three sides without the turning gap.

7 Turn right side out and push the corners into shape. Add stuffing and slip stitch the turning gap closed.

MAKE THE NEEDLEBOOK

8 Appliqué the felt leaves to the right-hand side of one needlebook exterior.

9 Stitch a soft strip of hook-and-loop tape to the left-hand side of the same piece. Save the matching "catchy" strip for the kit interior.

10 Pin the two fabric needlebook exterior pieces together, with right sides facing, and stitch, leaving the turning gap open as marked. Clip the corners and turn right side out. Push corners into shape and slip stitch the gap.

11 Fold the needlebook in half and crease along the middle to mark where to center the felt pages. Fold the felt pages in half, line up the fold with the crease, and topstitch along the crease on the outside of the needlebook.

motif & templates

enlarge 225%

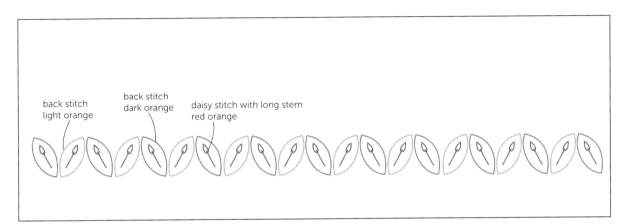

back stitch
light orange

back stitch
dark orange

daisy stitch with long stem
red orange

Kit exterior
cut 1 from felt

Kit interior
cut 1 from fabric

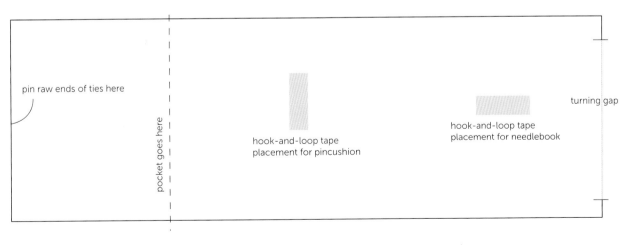

pin raw ends of ties here

pocket goes here

hook-and-loop tape
placement for pincushion

hook-and-loop tape
placement for needlebook

turning gap

full size PDF of motif & templates available on CD

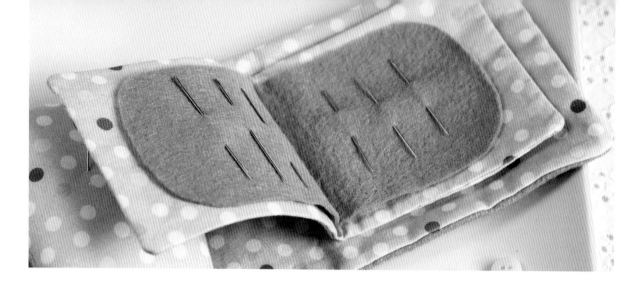

MAKE THE POCKET

12 Apply interfacing to the pocket, following manufacturer's directions, if you like it a bit more rigid.

13 Fold the pocket piece in half, right sides facing out. Topstitch along the folded edge once or twice, using a contrasting thread color, if you like.

MAKE THE TIES

14 Cut two pieces of bias tape, one 19½ inches (49.5 cm) long, and one 8½ inches (21.6 cm) long.

15 Open the bias tape and press under one end of each strip ¼ inch (6 mm). Stitch in place. Then refold the tape in half lengthwise and top stitch to close the open edges.

> **tip**
>
> A pretty ribbon can be substituted for the bias tape. If it is likely to fray, fold under and stitch one end of each strip to make a hem.

MAKE THE SEWING KIT

16 Press interfacing on the wrong side of the interior fabric (optional).

17 As indicated on the template, stitch the "catchy" hook-and-loop tape pieces (for the pincushion and the needlebook) on the right side of the interior fabric.

18 Transfer the motif to tissue paper. Baste the paper onto the felt kit exterior with the top of the motif 2 inches (5 cm) from the bottom edge.

19 Stitch the motif.

20 To assemble the kit, layer the elements like this:
* the kit interior fabric, right side up
* the pocket, right/topstitched side showing, at the left-hand edge
* both pieces of bias tape or ribbon, with the raw edges pinned as marked on the template
* the felt exterior, right side facing down

21 Pin everything and stitch together, leaving the turning gap as marked. When stitching, pay attention to where the bias tape is; it might move around as you work, so take care not to sew into it.

22 Clip the corners and turn right side out. Push the corners into shape, and slip stitch the turning gap closed.

23 Attach the pincushion and needlebook to the hook-and-loop tape patches.

templates

enlarge 225%

Pocket
cut 1 from fabric

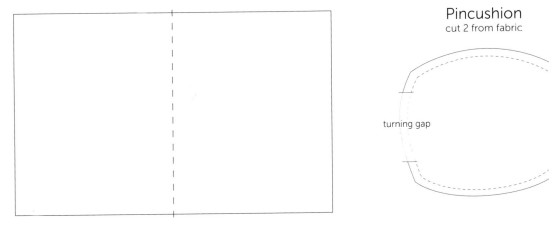

fold in half

Pincushion
cut 2 from fabric

turning gap

Needlebook exterior
cut 2 from fabric

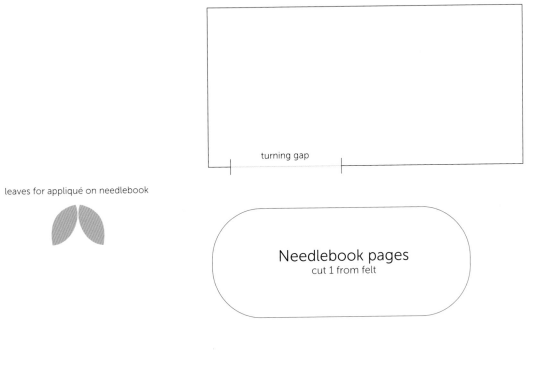

turning gap

leaves for appliqué on needlebook

Needlebook pages
cut 1 from felt

full size PDF of templates available on CD

sweet dreams bedding set

Flower petals scattered on a bed may look romantic in the movies, but probably aren't all that comfortable in reality. (And who cleans them up?) I'll take stitched flowers and petals any day!

you will need

- Motifs (page 75)
- Duvet and pillowcase for a single bed
- Transfer paper in a contrasting color, or a water-soluble fabric pen
- Seam ripper
- Sewing thread to match the color of the linen set
- 7- or 8-inch embroidery hoop (optional)
- Sewing machine (optional)

- Embroidery floss, 2 skeins each: bright pink*, powder pink*, cold pink*, burgundy, dark pink, pink, light pink, magenta, bubblegum pink, dark bubblegum pink, dark peach, light peach, pale blue, dark blue, light blue, medium blue, dark turquoise, medium turquoise, light turquoise

*I used satin threads S601, S899, and S602; they can be replaced with regular floss 601, 899, and 602.

I used DMC embroidery floss colors, 150, 600, 602, 603, 3804, 957, 956, 891, 893, 519, 995, 996, 3843, 3844, 3845, and 3846.

instructions

1 Mark the center of the pillowcase along its bottom edge, and mark the center of the duvet cover along its top or bottom edge, depending on your preference.

2 Enlarge the motifs by 300 percent, and transfer the "Pillow" part to the pillowcase and the "Duvet" part to the duvet cover using the transfer paper, starting at the center points you marked. The motifs are designed to extend from the center of each to the left, but you can easily reverse them if you like.

3 Rip out the seam from the center toward the motif side—not all the way, only as far as the pattern goes. It may seem a bit crazy to rip out the seam, but it will make it so much easier to stitch the pieces. Otherwise, you'd have a lot of fabric in the way and that's not very helpful.

4 Embroider the motifs. Once you're done, rinse off any transfer lines from the fabric and iron on the reverse when dry.

5 Turn the pillowcase and duvet cover wrong side out and sew the seams back together. You can do this with a sewing machine or by hand using the backstitch.

tips

* You can transfer the pattern by drawing it freehand. Don't worry if you make "mistakes"—that just means your pieces will be truly unique!
* If you want to use the pattern on a larger linen set, don't simply enlarge the pattern. Instead, draw it freehand and then extend the width of the branches on the duvet cover part and add more leaves, flowers, and swirly bits as you go.

motifs

enlarge 300%

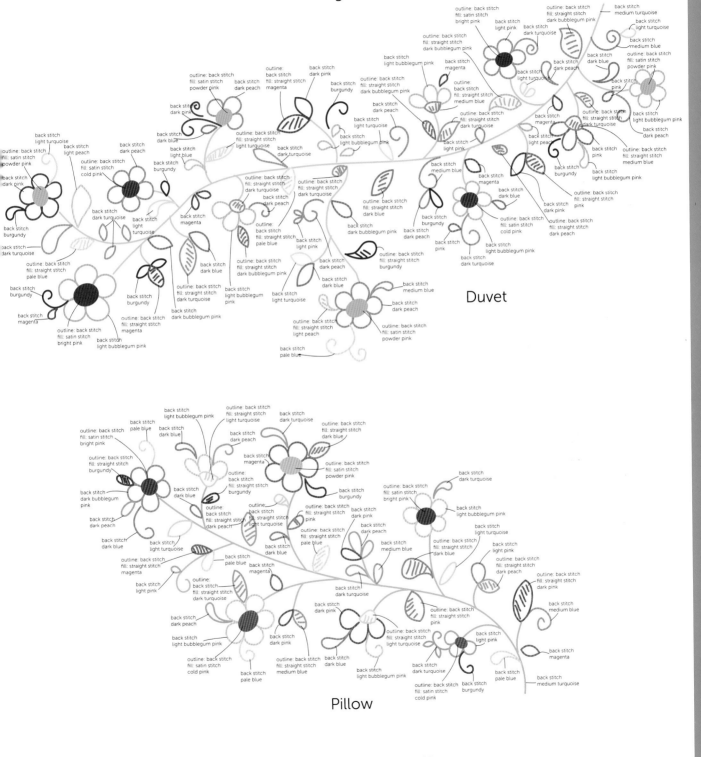

Duvet

Pillow

full size PDF of motifs available on CD

pj pocket pillow

Rise and shine! A clever pocket on the back of this pillowcase means no more excuses for throwing your PJs on the floor.

you will need

- Motif (page 78)
- 1 pillowcase, 19½ inches (49.5 cm) square; if using a different size, adjust the motif accordingly
- 1 piece of fabric measuring 19½ inches (49.5 cm) square
- 3 pieces of felt, each 6 inches (15.2 cm) square, in 3 different greens
- Embroidery floss, 1 skein each (match 3 of the floss colors to the green of the felt leaves; the remaining floss color should complement the others): yellow green, light green, kelly green, dark green

I used DMC perle cotton colors 704, 703, 702, and 700; you can use 3 strands of 6-strand floss, if you prefer.

instructions

STITCH THE EMBROIDERY

1 Enlarge the motif by 225 percent or, if using a different size pillowcase, enlarge to your liking. Trace and cut out the three felt leaf shapes.

2 Transfer the outlined leaves to the pillowcase.

3 Appliqué the felt leaves in place, and stitch the ribs inside them. You can do this freehand so they look more natural, or use the tissue paper method to transfer the lines (see page 18).

4 Stitch the outlined leaves.

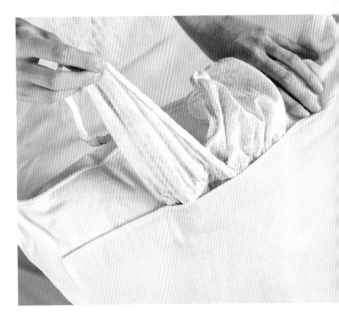

MAKE THE POCKET

5 Press under the fabric square 1 inch (2.5 cm) on all four sides. On one side, press under another 1 inch (2.5 cm); this will be the pocket opening. Pin the fold and topstitch two seams, ½ and ¾ inch (1.3 and 1.9 cm) from the folded edge.

6 Pin the pocket to the outside back of the pillowcase, with the opening edge of the pocket toward the top of the case.

7 Mark 5 inches (12.7 cm) from each corner at the opening edge. Starting at the right-hand mark, stitch clockwise around the pocket, ending at the left-hand mark. (Only stitch through the back of the pillow, of course!)

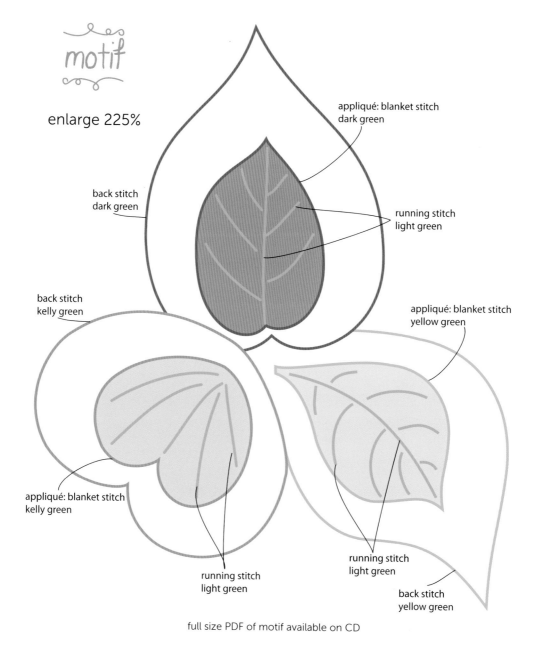

motif

enlarge 225%

back stitch
dark green

appliqué: blanket stitch
dark green

running stitch
light green

back stitch
kelly green

appliqué: blanket stitch
yellow green

appliqué: blanket stitch
kelly green

running stitch
light green

running stitch
light green

running stitch
light green

back stitch
yellow green

full size PDF of motif available on CD

english cottage tablecloth

Inspired by the table covering my grandmother embroidered for her summer cottage, this tablecloth adds enchantment to any dining area.

you will need

* Motifs (page 81)
* Tablecloth; round, square, or oblong are all good

* Embroidery floss, 1 skein each: dark bubblegum pink, pink, light orange, orange

I used DMC embroidery floss colors 956, 604, 741, and 970.

instructions

1 Enlarge the motifs by 150 percent. Transfer the larger version of the motif to the corners of the tablecloth.

2 In the center of the tablecloth, use a water-soluble fabric pen to draw a circle that is approximately 5 inches (12.7 cm) in diameter; use a cup or glass, this doesn't have to be exact.

3 Transfer the smaller version of the motif four times, evenly spaced around the circle. Position the motifs so that the point of each motif just touches the circle and the other end of it points toward the edge of the tablecloth.

4 Stitch the motifs.

5 Wash out the pen marks.

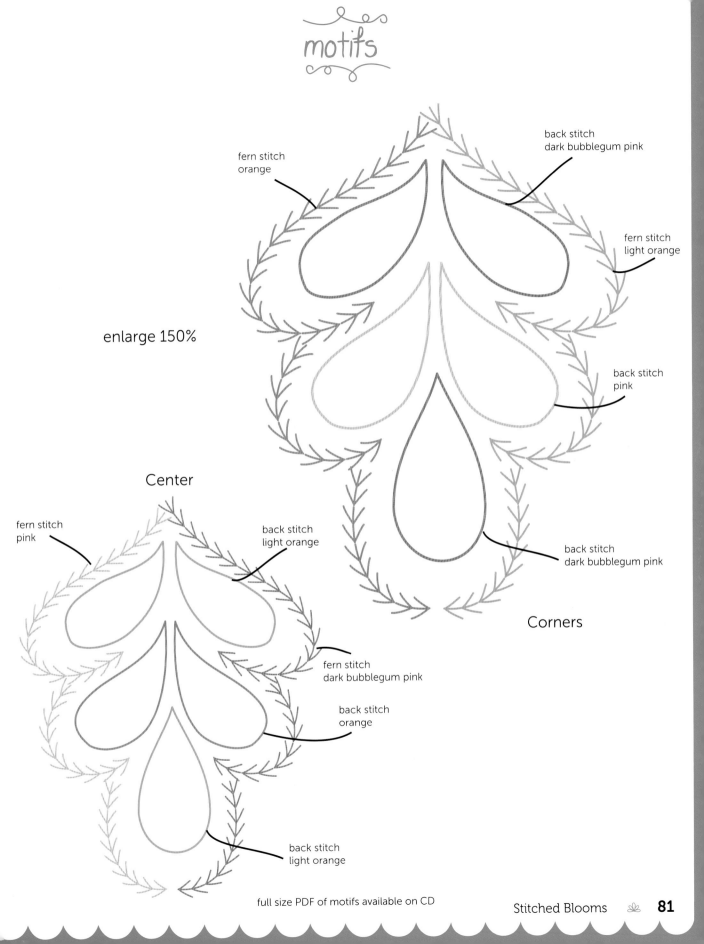

motifs

fern stitch orange

back stitch dark bubblegum pink

fern stitch light orange

enlarge 150%

back stitch pink

Center

fern stitch pink

back stitch light orange

back stitch dark bubblegum pink

Corners

fern stitch dark bubblegum pink

back stitch orange

back stitch light orange

full size PDF of motifs available on CD

Stitched Blooms

every day carry case

You'll never be without everything you need for the day—pens, keys, your trusty compact—when you corral them all in this handy little case.

you will need

* Templates and motif (page 84)
* 1 piece of teal cotton fabric, 16¾ x 7½ inches (42.5 x 19 cm)
* 1 piece of turquoise felt, same size as fabric
* 1 piece of interfacing, same size as fabric
* Hook-and-loop tape, 2-inch (5 cm) strip
* Embroidery floss, 1 skein each: pale green, mint, lilac, dark pink

I used DMC embroidery floss colors 772, 964, 210, and 602.

instructions

1 Enlarge the template by 400 percent. The template includes a ¼" (6mm) seam allowance. The motif is at 100 percent. Cut out the pieces of fabric, felt, and interfacing as indicated. Mark the turning gap on the felt piece.

2 Transfer the motif to the fabric exterior.

3 Stitch the motif.

4 Apply the interfacing to the wrong side of the exterior, following manufacturer's directions.

5 Sew half of the hook-and-loop tape on the fabric exterior and the other half on the felt interior, as indicated on the template.

6 Fold the exterior piece, with right sides facing, along the line indicated on the template. Fold the interior piece in the same way. Sew the straight side edges of each piece as shown on template. Leave open the turning gap on the interior piece.

7 Cut off the excess seam allowance, and clip the corners.

8 Turn the exterior piece right side out. Insert the exterior shell in the interior shell.

9 Sew the two pieces together along the straight edge of the opening, sewing right up to the side seams, but do not sew into or across the side seams.

10 Sew the pieces together along the curved edge of the opening, again starting and ending at the side seams but without sewing into them.

11 Notch along the curved edge. Turn the case right side out through the turning gap, so you see both the interior and exterior shell.

12 Push out the corners of the exterior so they are nice and sharp.

13 Slipstitch the turning gap on the interior and then push the interior felt shell inside the exterior fabric shell.

templates & motif

enlarge template 400%
motif is at 100%

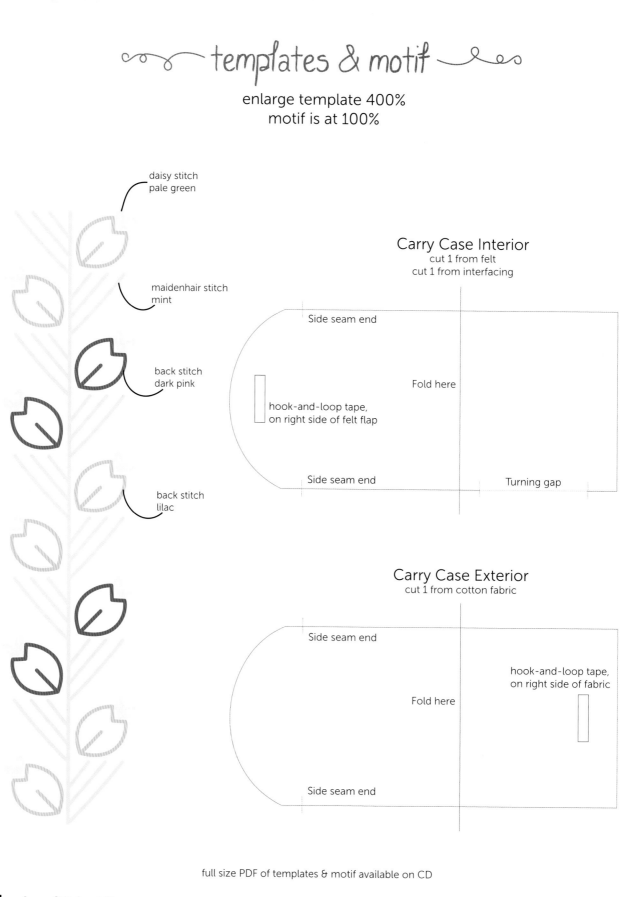

daisy stitch
pale green

maidenhair stitch
mint

back stitch
dark pink

back stitch
lilac

Carry Case Interior
cut 1 from felt
cut 1 from interfacing

Side seam end

Fold here

hook-and-loop tape,
on right side of felt flap

Side seam end

Turning gap

Carry Case Exterior
cut 1 from cotton fabric

Side seam end

hook-and-loop tape,
on right side of fabric

Fold here

Side seam end

full size PDF of templates & motif available on CD

mehndi tea towels

There is absolutely no reason why tea towels shouldn't look pretty, and even a simple design—like these mehndi-inspired patterns—will take a plain tea towel to a whole new level.

* Motifs (page 87)
* 2 tea towels
* Embroidery floss: 1 skein of white

I used DMC embroidery floss color blanc.

instructions

1 Enlarge the motifs to your liking. Transfer motif #1 diagonally in one corner of one tea towel, about ¾ inch (1.9 cm) from the edge of the hem. Transfer motif #2 to the corner of the other tea towel. The corner of motif #2 should be about 1 inch (2.5 cm) from the corner of the hem.

2 Stitch the motifs.

motifs

Motif #1

back stitch
white

running stitch
white

french knot
white

daisy stitch
white

back stitch
white

petal stitch
white

Motif #2

back stitch
white

running stitch
white

french knot
white

daisy stitch
white

french knot
white

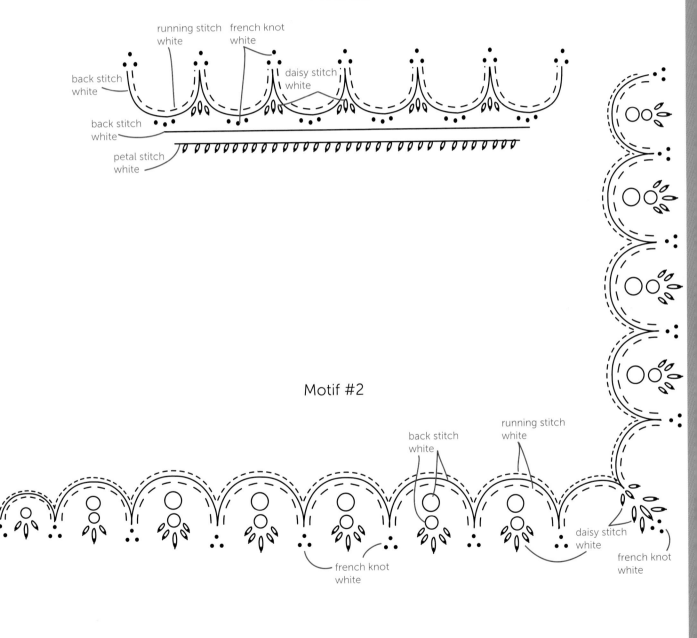

PDF of motifs available on CD

embroidered star shirt

Simple stars turn an ordinary shirt into
one that's uniquely yours.

you will need

- Motif (page 90)
- Shirt in your size

- Embroidery floss, 1 skein
  each: pale blue, light blue,
  dark blue, midnight blue

*I used DMC embroidery floss
colors 3753, 3755, 825, and
803.*

instructions

1 Size the motif to your liking, then center it
on the back of the shirt below the yoke, and
transfer it.

2 Stitch the motif.

3 Rinse off any transfer lines, let the shirt dry,
then press the shirt.

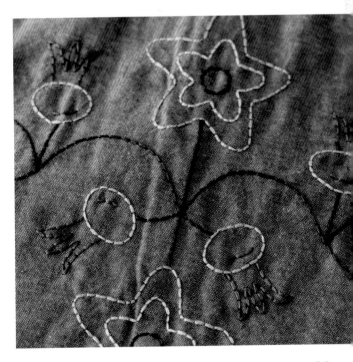

~ motif ~

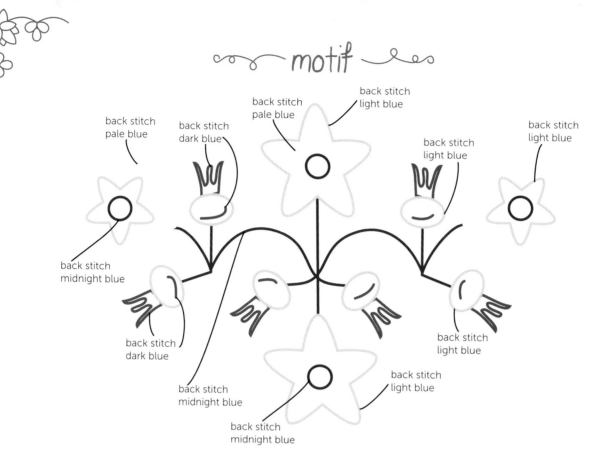

back stitch pale blue

back stitch dark blue

back stitch pale blue

back stitch light blue

back stitch light blue

back stitch light blue

back stitch midnight blue

back stitch dark blue

back stitch light blue

back stitch midnight blue

back stitch light blue

back stitch midnight blue

PDF of motif available on CD

pincushion petit fours

No more lost needles and pins in your couch cushions (ouch!).
Patterned after sweetly decorated cakes, these pincushions
look almost good enough to eat.

you will need

* Motifs (page 93)
* 2 pieces of fabric, 9 inches (22.9 cm) square
* Jello molds, 3 inches (7.6 cm) in diameter, or other cup or small bowl
* Stuffing

* Small bits of felt
* Glue that will bond the materials together (glue stick will not work for this)
* Embroidery floss, 1 skein each: yellow, light orange, dark bubblegum pink, pink

I used DMC embroidery floss colors 307, 741, 956, and 604.

instructions

1 In the middle of the piece of fabric, draw a circle by tracing around the top of your mold. Draw another circle inside the first one, about ¾ inch (1.9 cm) smaller in diameter.

2 Transfer a motif inside the smaller circle. Making the motif smaller than the diameter of the mold will prevent the stitches from being dragged down the sides too much.

3 Stitch the pattern and rinse off any transfer lines if necessary.

4 Draw and cut a large circle that just touches the sides of the fabric square. Hand-sew or machine-stitch basting stitches ⅓ inch (.8 cm) from the edge. Leave long tails at either end, and do not knot or fasten the thread at either end. If using a sewing machine, make another circle of stitches just inside the first one, taking care not to stitch into the first one. This will give you a better result.

5 Gather the circle by grabbing the thread ends and gently pulling. Adjust the gathers toward the middle as you go; they need to be evenly spaced. If you used a sewing machine, only pull the two spool threads.

6 When the fabric circle has become bowl-shaped, start stuffing it. Then pull it tighter still, adding more stuffing as necessary. Stuff it firmly, but not too firm, because it will be squeezed slightly when placed in the mold. Pull the threads tight, leaving a small gap in the center. Tie the threads together, and cut off the ends.

7 Test the pincushion in the mold. You may need to add more stuffing to make the gathers less pronounced. Don't worry if you can't get rid of all the creases completely—they just add character!

8 When you're happy with the pincushion, sew a small circle of felt over the hole. This will prevent the stuffing from falling out.

9 Glue the pincushion into the mold, following manufacturer's directions for the glue you're using.

Adapting the Design

If you want to make pincushions in vessels with different measurements, this is how you calculate how much fabric you'll need: Measure the diameter of the vessel and then multiply by 3. This is the length of the sides of the fabric pieces. If the vessel is very deep, compared to the diameter, then add another inch (2.5 cm) to each side.

motifs

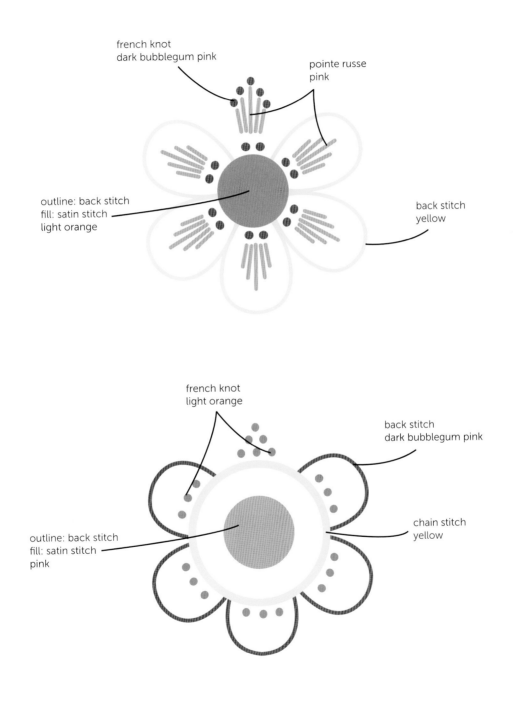

french knot
dark bubblegum pink

pointe russe
pink

outline: back stitch
fill: satin stitch
light orange

back stitch
yellow

french knot
light orange

back stitch
dark bubblegum pink

outline: back stitch
fill: satin stitch
pink

chain stitch
yellow

PDF of motifs available on CD

autumn night baby quilt

Appliqué works best with simple shapes, like the oak leaves and acorns on this quilt. And acorns are an ancient symbol of growth and good luck—perfect adornment in a nursery.

you will need

- Motifs (pages 96 and 97)
- Fabric for appliqué, each piece 10 inches (25.4 cm) square: egg yolk yellow, dark yellow, yellow orange, orange, lime green, olive, dark gold/goldenrod, dark brown
- 1 yard of fusible web
- White fabric for the top, 35 x 47 inches (88.9 x 119.4 cm)
- Fabric for back, 39 x 51 inches (99.1 x 129.5 cm)
- Batting/wadding, 39 x 51 inches (99.1 x 129.5 cm)

- 4¾ yards (4.3 m) of binding, 4 inches (10.2 cm) wide when unfolded
- Thread to quilt the quilt layers together
- Safety pins or special quilting safety pins
- Embroidery floss, 1 skein each to match the fabrics: egg yolk yellow, dark yellow, yellow orange, orange, lime green, olive, dark gold/goldenrod, dark brown, umber – for the branches

I used DMC embroidery floss colors 973, 833, 436, 721, 472, 166, 370, 938 and 420.

tip

Raw edge appliqué (page 24) is used for this quilt. If you want to use the needle-turn method instead (page 24), then you must add a ¼-inch (6 mm) seam allowance to each appliqué element.

instructions

APPLIQUÉ THE QUILT TOP

1 Apply fusible web to one side of the appliqué fabrics, following manufacturer's directions. It's a good idea to iron the fabrics first, to help avoid any creases when using the fusible web.

2 Enlarge the motifs by 400%. Transfer the acorn and leaf shapes to the interfaced fabrics, and cut them out.

3 Rinse off transfer lines if necessary.

4 On the right side of the quilt top:

* Mark 1½ inches (3.8 cm) from the center top edge and the same amount from each side edge. The horizontal motif will be placed within these bounds.
* Mark 1½ inches (3.8 cm) from the center bottom edge. Place the vertical motif here in the middle.

5 Using the enlarged motifs as a guideline, place the fabric leaves and acorns on the quilt top. Pin in place.

6 One by one, attach the acorns and leaves by peeling off the back from the fusible web and pressing each motif in place, following manufacturer's directions. Take care not to

iron on the transfer lines, as this could set them permanently.

7 Appliqué the motifs and chain stitch the branches.

8 Rinse out the transfer lines, and once dry iron all the motifs on the reverse of the quilt top.

ASSEMBLE THE QUILT

9 Layer the quilt as follows: the back (right side facing down), the batting, and the top (right side facing up). The top, which is smaller than the back and batting, should be centered on the other layers.

10 Pin the layers together at the center of the quilt and then move outward, smoothing the layers.

QUILT THE LAYERS

11 The quilting method used for this quilt is called tying. And the hint is in the name—you really do tie knots! Start by making marks across the base fabric with a water-soluble pen, 4 inches (10.2 cm) apart. If some of the marks are in the middle of a leaf or acorn, move the mark to the nearest spot on the base fabric. No one will ever know that you didn't follow the grid exactly!

12 For each mark you will need 4 inches (10.2 cm) of thread. Thread the needle but do not tie a knot. Pull the needle through from the back and make a short stitch over the mark you made. Push the needle to the back and tie the ends together 3 times. Cut off some of the ends so you have about ¾ inch (1.9 cm) left. Repeat for all the other marks. Bind the Quilt.

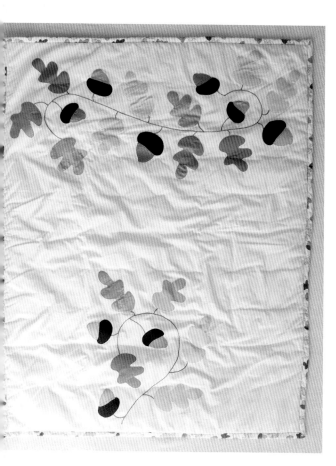

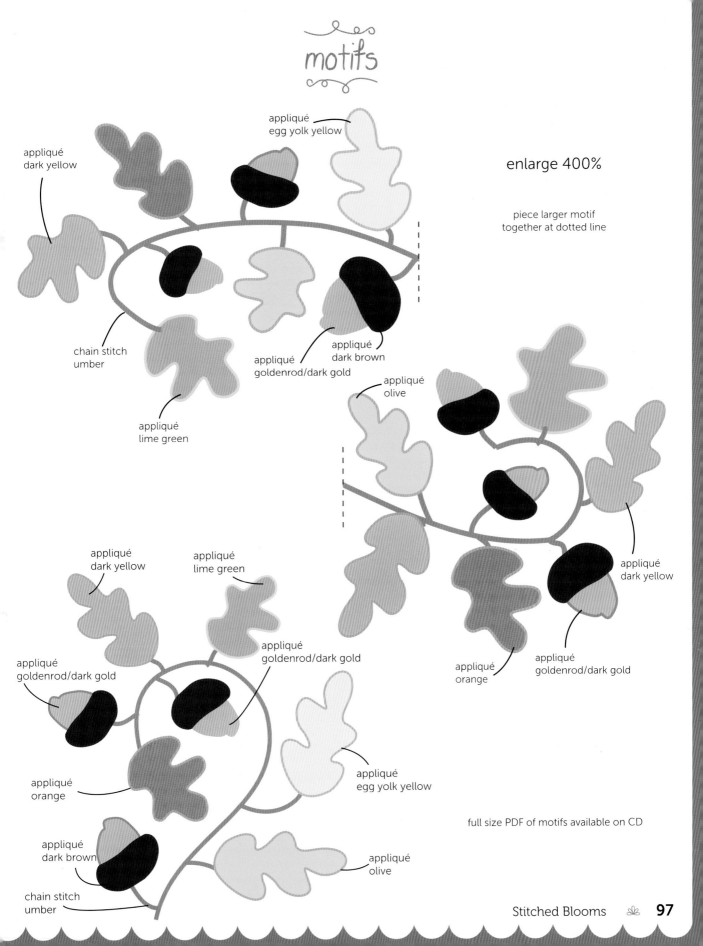

motifs

appliqué
egg yolk yellow

appliqué
dark yellow

enlarge 400%

piece larger motif
together at dotted line

chain stitch
umber

appliqué
goldenrod/dark gold

appliqué
dark brown

appliqué
olive

appliqué
lime green

appliqué
dark yellow

appliqué
dark yellow

appliqué
lime green

appliqué
goldenrod/dark gold

appliqué
goldenrod/dark gold

appliqué
orange

appliqué
goldenrod/dark gold

appliqué
orange

appliqué
egg yolk yellow

full size PDF of motifs available on CD

appliqué
dark brown

appliqué
olive

chain stitch
umber

13 Starting at the center of one side edge, pin the long raw edge of the binding to the edge of the quilt with right sides facing. When you get to a corner:

* Place a pin right in that corner but diagonally to the edge.
* Pinch the binding in the corner so a small triangular flap of fabric appears.
* Place another pin diagonally in the same corner but on the other side of this flap.
* Continue to pin the binding on the next side of the quilt, mitering the corners as you work. (see fig. A)

14 When you get back to where you started, make sure that the two ends of the binding overlap by 5 inches (12.7 cm), and cut off the excess.

15 Unpin a few inches (cm) of the start of the binding. Fold an inch (2.5 cm) of the end of the binding inside itself at an angle, and then tuck the start of the binding inside this fold. Pin in place. (see fig. B)

16 Stitch the binding in place, removing the pins as you go.

17 Fold the stitched binding to the back of the quilt, pin in place, and slip stitch the binding onto the back.

18 Remove all of the safety pins, and wash the quilt on a gentle cycle.

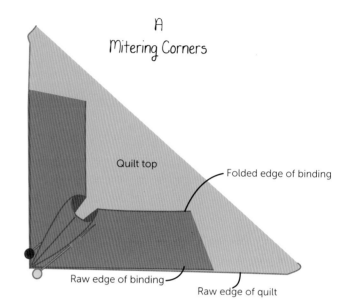

A
Mitering Corners

Quilt top

Folded edge of binding

Raw edge of binding

Raw edge of quilt

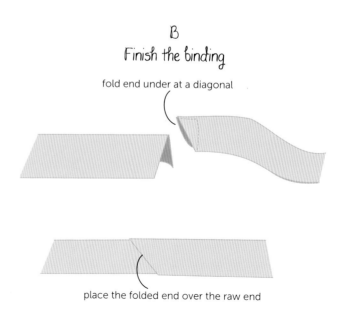

B
Finish the binding

fold end under at a diagonal

place the folded end over the raw end

mexican motif folk blouse

I've always loved the vivid colors and patterns on Mexican folk blouses. This pattern is my take on them. Add more motifs from the book to your own blouse to make it a truly unique piece in your wardrobe.

you will need

- Motif (page 101)
- A pretty blouse
- Transfer paper or water-soluble fabric pen
- Fabric stabilizer (optional)
- Pattern paper or printer paper

- Glue stick
- Embroidery floss, 1 skein each: yellow, light orange, orange, dark orange, orange red, pink, dark pink, pink lilac, purple, mint, grass green, apple green, yellow green

I used DMC embroidery floss colors 307, 972, 741, 608, 606, 602, 604, 210, 208, 954, 702, 907, and 3819.

instructions

1 Trace one half of the front of your blouse onto paper, along the shoulder, neckline, arm, and as far down the front as you'd like the stitching to go.

2 Copy or print out the motif template; you may need to resize it to find the best fit for your shirt size. Feel free to cut and move elements around to achieve the best layout on half of the blouse front. Once you're happy with the layout, glue the elements in place and make a copy.

3 Make a reversed copy of the finished pattern layout for the other half of the blouse. To do this, turn over the pattern layout and trace the motif onto another piece of paper. It may be easier to do this using a light table or a window. Use the same method as when transferring a pattern with a water soluble pen (page 18).

4 Tape the two halves together to make your finished pattern. If possible, make a photocopy of the whole pattern; otherwise, use your collage as a pattern.

5 If necessary, apply stabilizer to your fabric, following manufacturer's directions. If your stabilizer is the iron-on type, you must apply it before you transfer the pattern because the iron

can set the pattern transfer permanently! (See page 21 for more about stabilizers.)

6 Transfer the pattern to both halves of the blouse front.

7 Embroider the motifs.

8 Remove any stabilizer and leftover thread, and rinse out the transfer drawing. Once dry, gently iron the blouse on the reverse side.

motif

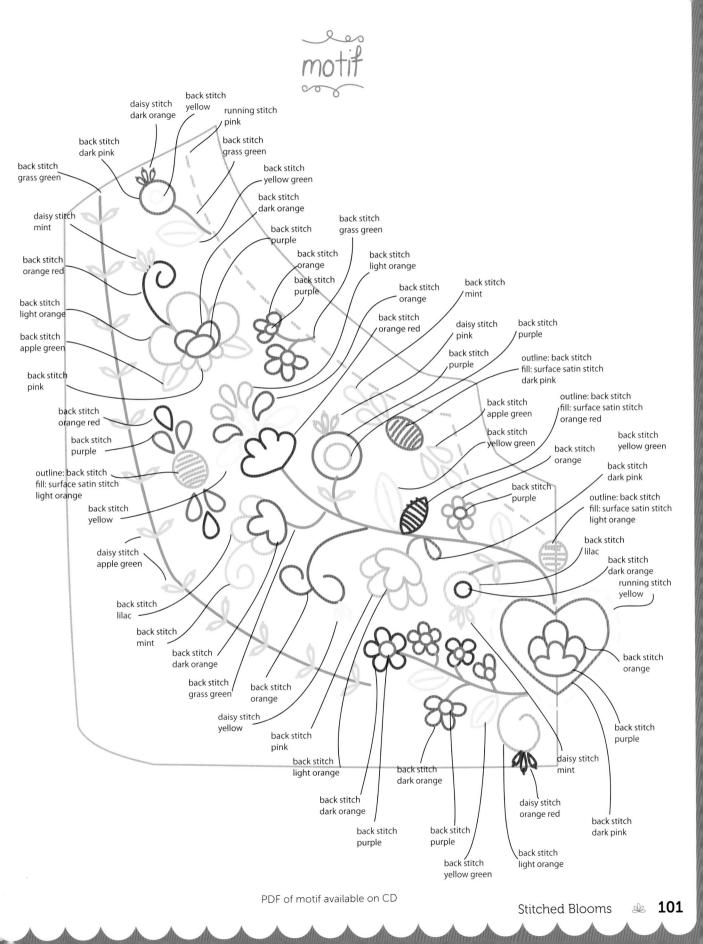

daisy stitch
dark orange

back stitch
yellow

running stitch
pink

back stitch
dark pink

back stitch
grass green

back stitch
grass green

back stitch
yellow green

daisy stitch
mint

back stitch
dark orange

back stitch
purple

back stitch
grass green

back stitch
orange red

back stitch
orange

back stitch
light orange

back stitch
light orange

back stitch
purple

back stitch
orange

back stitch
apple green

back stitch
orange red

back stitch
mint

back stitch
pink

back stitch
orange red

daisy stitch
pink

back stitch
purple

back stitch
orange red

daisy stitch
purple

back stitch
purple

outline: back stitch
fill: surface satin stitch
dark pink

outline: back stitch
fill: surface satin stitch
orange red

back stitch
yellow

back stitch
apple green

back stitch
yellow green

back stitch
orange

back stitch
yellow green

outline: back stitch
fill: surface satin stitch
light orange

back stitch
purple

back stitch
purple

back stitch
dark pink

daisy stitch
apple green

outline: back stitch
fill: surface satin stitch
light orange

back stitch
lilac

back stitch
lilac

back stitch
dark orange

back stitch
mint

running stitch
yellow

back stitch
dark orange

back stitch
grass green

back stitch
orange

back stitch
orange

daisy stitch
yellow

back stitch
pink

back stitch
purple

back stitch
light orange

back stitch
dark orange

back stitch
dark orange

back stitch
purple

back stitch
purple

daisy stitch
mint

back stitch
yellow green

daisy stitch
orange red

back stitch
light orange

back stitch
dark pink

The project section of this book contains 33 motifs; in this section, you'll find an additional colorful and fun 267! You can print them out from these pages in any size you'd like, then mix and match them to suit your own projects. Or, download black and white versions from the enclosed CD. All EPS files can be rotated, cropped, and edited; JPEG files can be used as is. Let your imagination guide you, and enjoy!

BORDERS & CORNERS

001

002

003

004

005

006

007

008

009

010

011

BORDERS & CORNERS

012

013

014

015

016

017

018

019

020

021

022

BORDERS & CORNERS

023

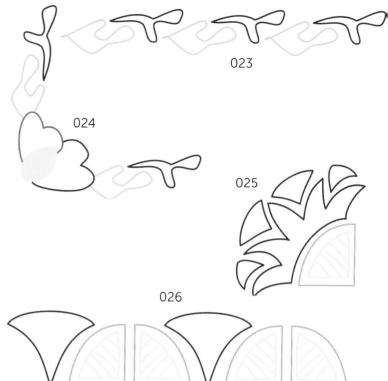

024

025

027

026

028

030

031

032

029

033

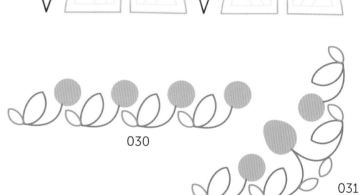

034

035

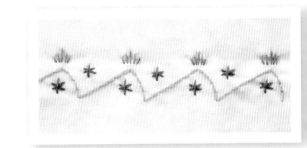

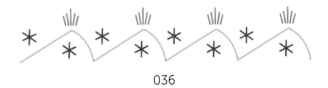

036

037

038

039

040

041

042

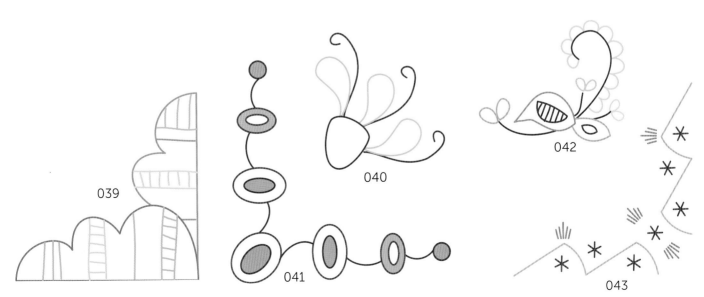

043

FOLK ART BLOOMS

044

045

046

047

048

049

050

051

052

053

054

055

056

057

058

059

FOLK ART BLOOMS

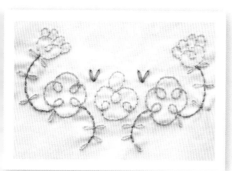

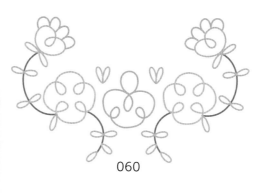

060

061

062

063

064

065

066

068

069

067

070

071

072

073

074

075

076

077

078

079

080

081

FOLK ART BLOOMS

082

083

084

085

086

087

088

089

090

091

092

093

094

095

096

097

098

099

100

101

102

FOLK ART BLOOMS

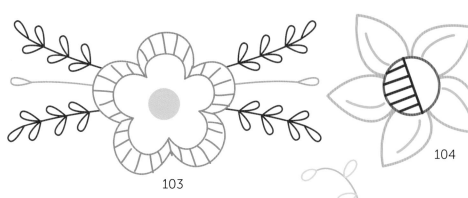

103

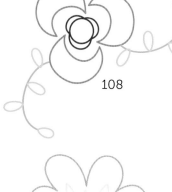

104

106

107

108

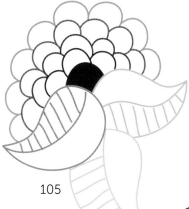

105

109

110

111

113

114

112

115

116

117

119

120

118

121

122

123

BOLD & BEAUTIFUL BLOOMS

124

125

126

127

128

129

130

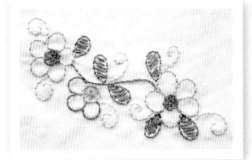

131

132

133

134

135

136

137

LEAFY BLOOMS

138

139

140

141

142

143

144

145

146

147

148

149

150

151

152

153

154

155

156

157

158

159

160

161

162

163

MINIMALIST BLOOMS

164

165

166

167

168

169

170

171

172

173

174

175

176

177

178

179

180

181

182

183

184

185

NATURE'S BLOOMS

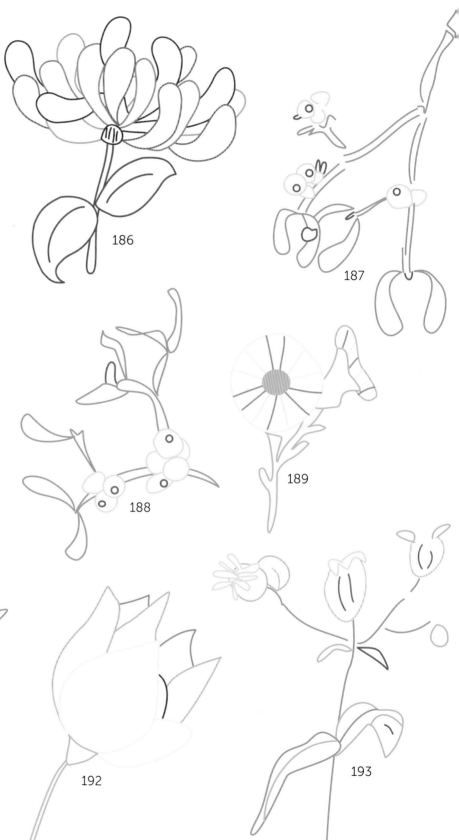

186

187

188

189

190

191

192

193

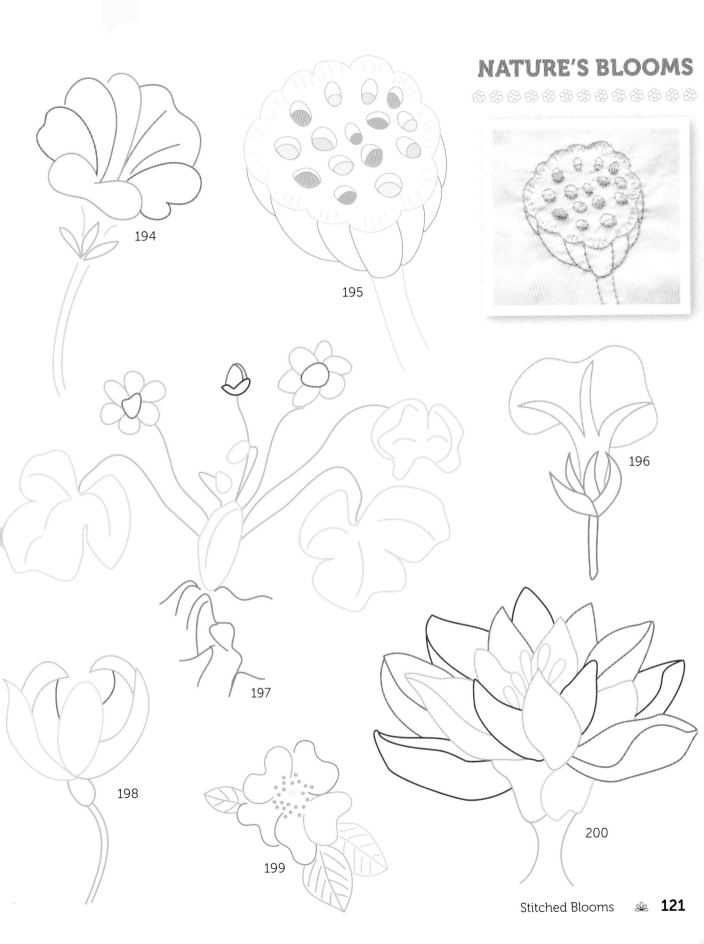

194

195

196

197

198

199

200

NATURE'S BLOOMS

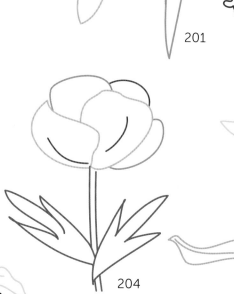

201

202

203

204

205

206

207

208

209

210

211

212

213

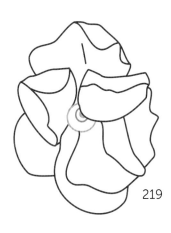

214

215

216

217

218

219

SMALL & SWEET BLOOMS

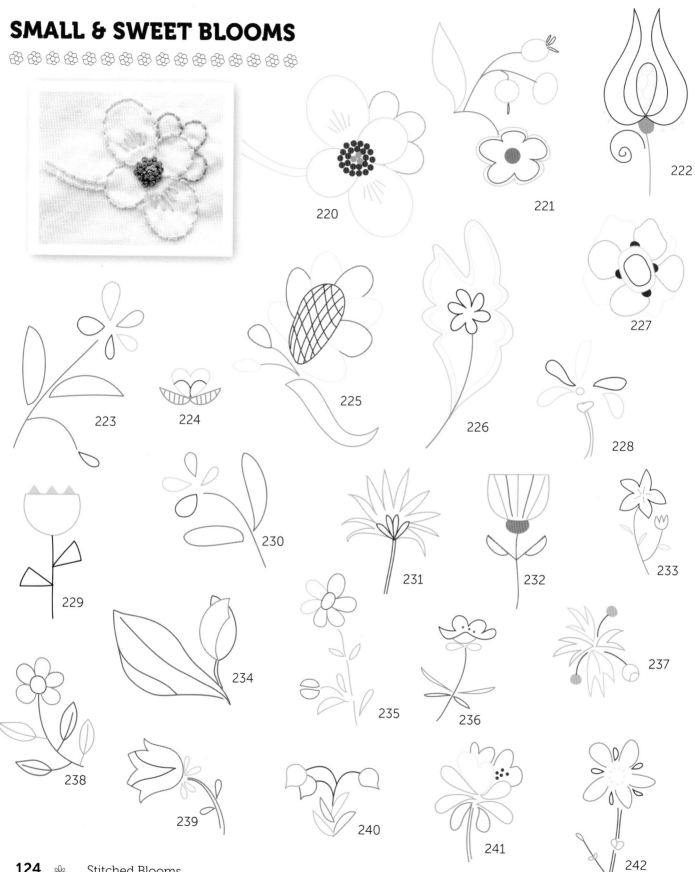

220

221

222

223

224

225

226

227

228

229

230

231

232

233

234

235

236

237

238

239

240

241

242

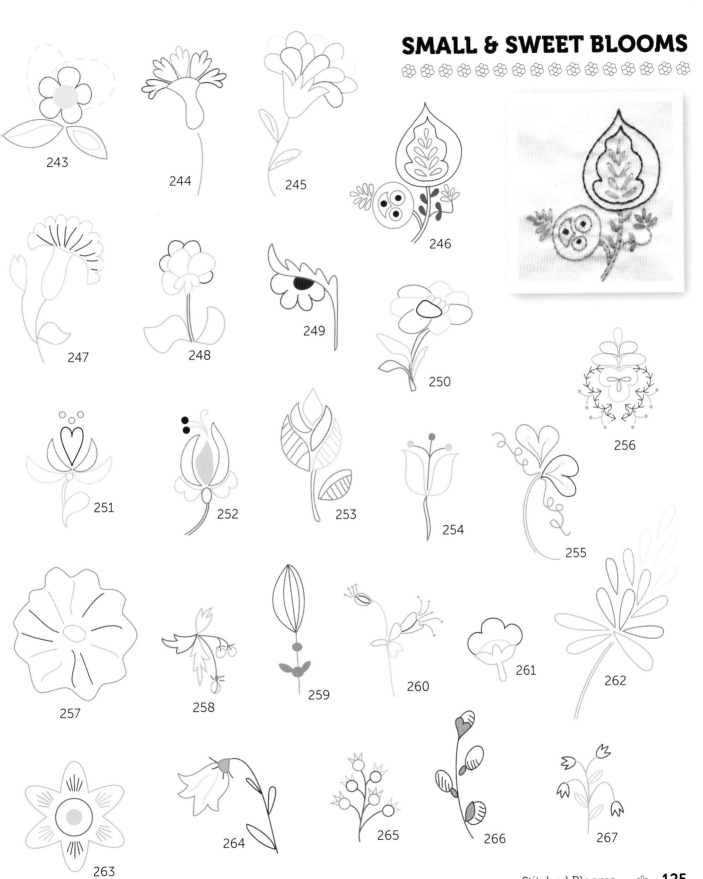

SMALL & SWEET BLOOMS

243

244

245

246

247

248

249

250

251

252

253

254

255

256

257

258

259

260

261

262

263

264

265

266

267

Calendar Insert

Month

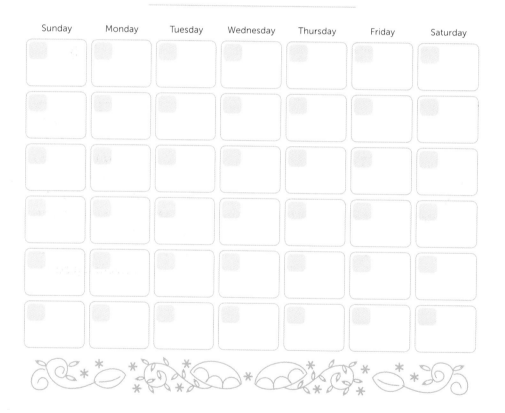

Sunday	Monday	Tuesday	Wednesday	Thursday	Friday	Saturday

PDF of insert available on CD

Acknowledgments

Dedication

For Tony, my sweet husband and chief loose-threads-off-the-floor picker. For farmor (my paternal grandmother) who was a Crafty Superstar, but would never have thought of herself that way!

Gratitude

To mor & far (mom & dad) for always encouraging my creative pursuits and not minding too much about going to a lot of (art) museums when I was too young to go/pay for it by myself. To mor, especially, for her expert skills in sewing some of the projects in this book, for not minding the countless phone calls about this book and for passing on her passion for sewing. To my editors, Amanda Carestio, who set this book process in motion, and Shannon Quinn-Tucker who have both offered great encouragement and inspiration throughout, thank you so much! To my excellent agent, Kate McKean at Howard Morhaim Literary Agency for answering all my many questions with great clarity and patience.

To the following for generously contributing materials for the book:

* pixierose.co.uk for supplying me with gorgeous felt used throughout the book
* Susie Stubbs of www.flowerpress.com.au for sending me the 'Hundreds and Thousands in Violet' fabric used in the sewing kit project on page 67
* Michelle of www.michellepatterns.com for giving me permission to use the 'Belted Tote Bag' pattern to make the bag on page 56 http://keyka.typepad.com/my_weblog/belted-tote-bag-pdf-sewing-pattern.html

To my testers: Jo Stafferton, Carolyn Grill, Cynthia Gould. And especially Anne Gregory for being a tester extraordinaire! To Nicole Vos van Avezathe and Julie Zaichuk-Ryan for all your help! June Gilbank and Diane Gilleland for your friendship and great advice. You rock! Last, but definitely not least, to the readers of my blog, Carina's Craftblog, and the Polka & Bloom customers: thank you! I can never adequately express how much your support means to me!

About the Author

Carina Envoldsen-Harris is a designer, blogger, and author. Originally from Denmark, she now lives just outside London, UK, with her English husband. Carina has been making things for as long as she can remember—painting, drawing, and embroidering. Under the name Polka & Bloom, she creates colorful embroidery patterns and fabric designs. You can see more of her work on her blog: carinascraftblog.com.

Index

Editors: Shannon Quinn-Tucker
  and Amanda Carestio
Art Director: Shannon Yokeley
Graphic Designer: Raquel Joya
Illustrator: Carina Envoldsen-Harris
Photographers: S. Stills,
  Carina Envoldsen-Harris
Cover Designer: Raquel Joya,
  Shannon Yokeley